Understanding and
Reaching New Agers

CRYSTAL CLEAR

● ● ● ● ● ● ● ● ● ● ● ● ● ● ● ● ● ●

A Small Group Discussion Guide

DEAN C. HALVERSON

D1405380

NAVPRESS (◢)®
A MINISTRY OF THE NAVIGATORS
P.O. BOX 6000, COLORADO SPRINGS, COLORADO 80934

The Navigators is an international Christian
organization. Jesus Christ gave His followers
the Great Commission to go and make
disciples (Matthew 28:19). The aim of The
Navigators is to help fulfill that commission by
multiplying laborers for Christ in every nation.

NavPress is the publishing ministry of The
Navigators. NavPress publications are tools
to help Christians grow. Although publications alone cannot make disciples or change
lives, they can help believers learn biblical
discipleship, and apply what they learn to their
lives and ministries.

© 1990 by Dean C. Halverson
All rights reserved, including translation
ISBN 08910-93109

All Scripture quotations in this publication
are from the *Holy Bible: New International
Version* (NIV). Copyright © 1973, 1978, 1984,
International Bible Society. Used by permission
of Zondervan Bible Publishers.

Printed in the United States of America

CONTENTS

To my beautiful wife,
Debbie

AUTHOR

Dean C. Halverson is the World Religions Specialist for International Students, Inc., a Christian organization headquartered in Colorado Springs, Colorado, that ministers to undergraduate and graduate-level international students. Before joining ISI in 1987, Dean worked for eight years as a researcher and writer with the Spiritual Counterfeits Project in Berkeley, California. Through SCP, Dean published a number or articles on New Age-related groups and teachings, and contributed two chapters to *The New Age Rage* (Revell, 1987).

Dean lives in Colorado Springs with his wife, Debbie, and three children.

WHAT IS THE NEW AGE?

Warm-up

In the next few pages we will ask and briefly answer the question, "What is the New Age?" After opening your session with prayer, give everyone in the group a chance to introduce himself and complete this sentence: "To me, the term *New Age* brings to mind. . . ."

Next, have one or two people read the following information aloud. As they read, think about this question: How have you seen these ideas influencing your community or the people you know?

Identifying the New Age

Humanity stands at the threshold of a new millennium. Those in the New Age movement believe that we also stand at the brink of a new spiritual era. They promise a new world through personal and social transformation, and the hope of that promise is catching on in our culture.

What is the New Age? Most fundamentally, it is a belief system. What do New Agers believe?[1] New Age thought includes three major themes: God is cosmic energy, humanity is divine, and humanity's purpose is to transform itself through spiritual awareness.

God Is Cosmic Energy. All New Age practices revolve around manipulating or tapping into some form of energy, whether

7

it is characterized as psychic, consciousness, mind, light, life force, or an aura. New Agers identify that energy as God, and they consider God an impersonal oneness that is beyond all distinctions.

Humanity Is Divine. Since New Agers say we are extensions of this underlying God energy, they perceive humanity as divine. Because of this innate connection, an infinite amount of unrealized potential exists within us.

Humanity's Purpose. According to New Agers, humanity's purpose is to realize that inner divinity and then utilize it through some spiritual technique to transform ourselves and the world. Many environmental, political, and social problems plague the world and indicate that humanity as a whole is doing something wrong. The New Age movement says that the only hope for humanity's survival is through a fundamental change in the way we see ourselves and the universe. We need a new world view, a new perception, a new paradigm. That new world view consists of the realization of our divinity and the interconnectedness of all things. If a person were looking for an attitude that hits close to the heart of what the New Age is all about, the following would not be far from the mark: New Agers believe that we each have the potential within to transform ourselves and thereby the world.

After those three major themes, there are several subthemes. First, New Agers believe the mind has tremendous power. Second, they believe in the inherent goodness of humanity. Third, they believe that truth is relative and that there are many paths to God. Fourth, the holistic perspective guides their approach to everything, including education, health, and politics.

The New Age movement is not a quirk of history, but in fact flows from several other movements, including transcendentalism, Eastern religions, secular humanism, occultism, spiritism, New Thought, Theosophy, and the sixties counterculture.

The New Age movement is a strong influence in our culture. As *Time* magazine reported in 1987, Bantam Books increased its New Age titles tenfold in the previous ten years, and the number of New Age bookstores doubled in the last five.[2] In 1982, a Gallup poll reported that 23 percent of all Americans believed in reincarnation. The New Age movement is a network of separate movements and people within those movements. Through these individual movements, the New Age movement has influenced every aspect of society, including psychology, medicine, music, sports, science, religion, and education.

1. Share an experience you have had with the New Age or a New Ager. (If you can't think of any, read through the questions on pages 10-11.)

2. Think about the description of the New Age given earlier and discuss where you have seen the influence of the New Age in your community. Consider:

   ■ schools
   ■ the workplace
   ■ television and movies
   ■ newspapers and other literature
   ■ local events

3. How have your encounters with the New Age made you feel about the New Age in general or about New Agers in particular?

Ways to Detect New Age Influence
When it comes to discerning the influence of the New Age movement, the primary issue to focus on is the world view that stands behind a particular technique or teaching. Make no mistake about this: The New Age movement is a religion

based on monistic (all is one) and pantheistic (all is God) perspectives. In such a belief system, God's otherness is denied and His withinness is emphasized.

When God's otherness is denied and His withinness affirmed, we tend to put man in the place of God and to attribute to humanity the characteristics that were previously reserved for God. For example, Lifespring, a human-potential group, speaks of the individual as being "perfect," as having "unlimited potential and knowledge," and as having the power to determine and shape his reality so much that he is totally responsible for everything that happens to him. (See page 63.)

As another example, several editors of the *New Age Journal* summarized what they saw as the two most important ideas for maintaining healthy relationships: (1) realize that "we are all one," and that we "come from the same [divine] source"; and (2) realize "that each of us is whole, complete, and perfect—exactly as we are. All that we need is contained within us."[3]

The following are some questions to ask if you think you see the influence of the New Age belief system in the school curriculum, books, media, job training seminars, or the person next door.

■ **Is humanity spoken of in extremely optimistic terms, such as having unlimited potential?**
■ **Is guilt talked about as being nothing more than a matter of the mind?**
■ **Is the objectivity (otherness) of reality so diminished that a person's subjective perception becomes the central factor in seeing reality?**
■ **Are you being told that all religions are in their essence the same?**
■ **Is your previous belief system called "limiting" or "reductionistic"? Are you being encouraged to replace it with a new, more expansive one? (See the glossary for definitions of New Age terms that might be unfamiliar.)**
■ **Does the teaching or technique divert you from**

trusting in a personal, transcendent God and encourage you to depend on some power within yourself, such as the power of your mind or your ability to visualize something into reality?

■ Do you sense that the technique being recommended promises too much?

■ Are you being encouraged to quiet or still your mind by the repetition of a syllable or phrase, by sensory deprivation, or by concentrating on controlling your breathing?

■ Are traditionally Eastern religious concepts, words, or techniques being used, such as mantra, OM, yoga, karma, reincarnation, or chakras?

■ Are various forms of energy—light, consciousness, life force, psychic power, or aura—mentioned? Are they spoken of as being universal and ultimate?

■ Are words such as *universe* and *nature* capitalized to imply ultimacy?

■ Is the earth personified, spoken of as a living, conscious being?

■ Are you being encouraged to mentally cultivate the image of beings you might encounter through guided imagery or dream work? Are you being told to seek the wisdom of these beings because their wisdom is beyond yours?

4. (Optional) How do the above questions help you deal with or understand the situations you named in questions 1 and 2? (For instance, which questions would you answer "yes"?)

5. From what you know of the New Age movement thus far, why do you suppose people are attracted to it?

6. Think about the following incident. Your son tells you

during supper that in his math class that day his teacher stopped teaching in the middle of the period, sat on his desk in the lotus position, and asked a student to turn the lights off. In a monotone voice, he had the class close their eyes and meditate on the word *OM*. Then he had them repeat Pythagorean theorems for a few minutes. They ended by meditating on OM for a while longer. The session lasted a total of ten minutes.

What would be the Christlike steps to take in such a situation? You might consider how 1 Peter 3:15-16 applies in this situation: "But in your hearts set apart Christ as Lord. Always be prepared to give an answer to everyone who asks you to give the reason for the hope that you have. But do this with gentleness and respect, keeping a clear conscience, so that those who speak maliciously against your good behavior in Christ may be ashamed of their slander."

NOTES
1. "New Age" is an increasingly common term. The secular press uses it, but many followers of New Age ideas consider it a condescending label. I use it for convenience here, but you'd be unwise to call someone a New Ager if you want him to feel that you respect or love him.
2. Otto Friedrich, et al., "New Age Harmonies," *Time,* vol. 130, no. 23 (December 7, 1987), pages 62-72.
3. Rick Fields, et al., eds., *Chop Wood, Carry Water* (Los Angeles, CA: J. P. Tarcher, 1984), page 37.

SESSION TWO

THE CHRISTIAN RESPONSE

At its core, the New Age philosophy is incompatible with
Christianity. There is a place, therefore, for analyzing and bib-
lically critiquing the New Age belief system and identifying
its influence in our culture. As Christians we must sound a
warning concerning the false hope that the New Age offers. We
must be careful, though, that the attitude of separation involved
in critiquing the New Age belief system doesn't interfere with
building a relationship with the New Ager next door.

The Church has been slow to view the New Age movement as a mission field and to mobilize its members into action.
We as Christians need to give more thought on how to effectively share the gospel with those in the New Age movement.

To some Christians, sharing the gospel comes naturally;
to many, it doesn't.

1. As I think about making friends with New Agers and
   introducing them to Jesus, my gut feeling is:

   a. what fun!
   b. panic
   c. disgust
   d. ambivalence
   e. guilt
   f. indifference
   g. other: _____

2. Why do you feel that way? [10 minutes]

3. (Optional) Give everyone a chance to describe one positive experience he or she has had in sharing the gospel.

4. Who introduced you to the Lord? What made them qualified to share the gospel with you? Were they specially trained to do so?

5. Sharing Christ with New Agers takes practice, and the more we practice, the more confident we will become. How do the following words of Scripture pertain to the fears and concerns that you might have about evangelism?

Pray also for me, that whenever I open my mouth, words may be given me so that I will fearlessly make known the mystery of the gospel, for which I am an ambassador in chains. Pray that I may declare it fearlessly, as I should. (Ephesians 6:19-20)

For this reason I remind you to fan into flame the gift of God, which is in you through the laying on of my hands. For God did not give us a spirit of timidity, but a spirit of power, of love and of self-discipline. So do not be ashamed to testify about our Lord. (2 Timothy 1:6-8)

"Therefore go and make disciples of all nations, baptizing them in the name of the Father and of the Son and of the Holy Spirit, and teaching them to obey everything I have commanded you. And surely I am with you always, to the very end of the age." (Matthew 28:19-20)

Breaking Down the Stereotypes

There is a comparatively large New Age population in the city in which I live, and they hold two to three New Age fairs each year. At the last fair, several Christians gathered around the entrances to hand out tracts. It was rather obvious they were Christians, since two of them were carrying ten-foot-tall wooden crosses. The police were there, too, because the organizers of the fair had called and complained that the Christians were blocking the entrances to the auditorium.

I quietly walked into the auditorium and began to browse around the booths. As I browsed, I struck up conversations with several of those who were manning the booths. Posing as an objective observer, I asked questions about the theories behind whatever they were selling, whether it was yoga, algae pills, soul travel, light therapy, or crystals. Their answers inevitably led our conversation to spiritual matters. My goals for such conversations are to begin a relationship that can be continued through letters or personal meetings and gently provoke their thinking, especially with respect to the issue of whether God is personal or impersonal.

I've found that gentle persuasion based on a personal relationship is more effective than confrontation and preaching.

New Agers have stereotypes of Christians in their minds, and often we enforce those stereotypes. My experience has been that New Agers are somewhat shocked when they meet a Christian who shows respect and love for them as individuals and is able to talk reasonably about spiritual matters.

6. What are some of the stereotypes that you think New Agers have of Christians?

7. In 1 Corinthians 9:22, Paul revealed a guiding principle that determined his method of evangelism: "I have become all things to all men so that by all possible means I might save some." Often we as Christians focus on minor issues and allow them to prevent us from building a relationship with a New Ager.

a. Read 1 Corinthians 9:19-23. What principle can we draw from this paragraph?

b. How can we apply it to reaching New Agers for Christ?

8. a. What should our primary concern be when attempting to evangelize a New Ager?

b. What are some minor issues that might detour us?

Project for the Week: Ask a New Ager how he views Christians in general.

The Genuine Good News

Paul exhorts Timothy to "do the work of an evangelist" (2 Timothy 4:5). "Good news" is the literal meaning of the Greek word from which "evangelist" is derived. A Christian evangelist, then, is one who is devoted to proclaiming the good news of Jesus Christ.

In that same passage, though, Paul warns Timothy that people will reject sound doctrine and "will gather around them a great number of teachers to say what their itching ears want to hear" (4:3). That which we want to hear will always sound like good news to us. In this one chapter, then, two opposing forms of good news appear. How are we to know which is the best news? By asking, "Where is the bad news?"

While the New Age movement begins with good news, it ends with bad news. Christianity, on the other hand, begins with bad news but ends with good news. Christianity, then, has genuine good news, while the good news of the New Age will disappoint in the end.

Throughout the following chapters, we'll look at this good news/bad news theme in both Christianity and the New Age, so you will be better prepared to have friendly, reasonable conversations with the New Agers you encounter. It is interesting to note how this bad news/good news theme is rather explicit in a couple of Bible verses:

> For the wages of sin is death, but the gift of God is eternal life in Christ Jesus our Lord. (Romans 6:23)

> Once you were alienated from God and were enemies in your minds because of your evil behavior. But now he has reconciled you by Christ's physical body through death to present you holy in his sight, without blemish and free from accusation. (Colossians 1:21-22)

9. Have several people share, in their own words, the bad news and the good news of the Christian gospel.

10. Paul wrote, "The god of this age has blinded the minds of unbelievers, so that they cannot see the light of the gospel of the glory of Christ, who is the image of God" (2 Corinthians 4:4). What has the god of this age used to blind New Agers?

Take a few minutes to pray together for the people you know who are involved in the New Age. You may or may not want to name those people. Ask God to open their eyes and hearts so they can understand the genuine good news of Jesus Christ. Pray for the gentleness and respect you need in order to talk with them. Pray also for an authentic love for such people.

THE GOD
OF THE NEW AGE

Warm-up
Before you read this section, give everyone a chance to answer the following question (limit each answer to one minute): If you had to describe God to someone who knew nothing about Him, what would you say?

Is God a Person?
One young lady approached me after a talk I had given on the New Age and said, "I don't believe God is a person, and I don't believe He will judge us, and I don't believe we have only one chance."[1] I pointed out to her that she had just denied God's personhood while affirming it at the same time by referring to Him with the personal pronoun *He.* She responded, "Well, how do you want me to refer to God?"

I said, "If you're going to be consistent, you should refer to God as an *it.*" She complied, and after we talked for a while longer, she said that referring to God as an "it" just didn't feel right. I agreed.

New Agers are inconsistent in that while they deny God's personhood, they use personal attributes to describe Him. In *The Aquarian Conspiracy,* for example, Marilyn Ferguson wrote, "In the emergent spiritual tradition God is not the personage of our Sunday-school mentality. . . . God is experienced as flow, wholeness . . . the ground of being. . . . God is the consciousness that manifests as *lila,* the play of the universe. God is the organizing matrix we can experience but not tell, that which enlivens matter."[2] In that statement, Ferguson denies that God is personal, but she still attributes personal characteristics to Him. What, after all, is more conscious, more rational (or "organizing"), and more alive than a person?

Let's explore the ramifications of the question of God's personhood.

1. Let's say that God is like an ocean of consciousness (or energy, or life force, or whatever) and that this ocean is all there is. Nothing else exists. You are an individual portion of that ocean, but you falsely believe you are separate from its vast expanse. You are like a drop of water that has been whipped up by the wind and temporarily suspended above the ocean. You fear, though, that your separation is permanent.

   a. What is the goal of the individual person—the supposedly separate self—in the context of such a God?

   b. Would moral issues be involved in knowing God? Why or why not?

2. Now think of God as a loving Father who has laid down certain laws in the home and expects you to abide by them. Out of defiance, you have deliberately broken several of those laws.

   a. Are moral issues involved in knowing God? Why or why not?

   b. What does your act of rebellion do to your relationship with your Father?

   c. What would it take to restore your relationship with such a God?

3. In light of these two different concepts of God, what is humanity's primary problem if . . .

God is impersonal?

God is personal?

The Meaning of Love

Both New Agers and Christians would agree with the statement that "God is love" (1 John 4:8), but they mean two different things when they say that.

New Ager Stuart Wilde wrote, "The Force loves you."[3] He also says, "In fact, pain and suffering are not part of God's plan. They are factors of the coarseness of the vibrational field of the physical plane. *The Force is not involved. It does not even have an immediate awareness of the negativity.*"[4]

Shirley MacLaine wrote, "God is love—which is *the highest vibrational frequency of all.*"[5]

The author of Hebrews writes of Jesus, God's Son, "For we do not have a high priest who is unable to sympathize with our weaknesses, but we have one who has been tempted in every way, just as we are—yet was without sin" (Hebrews 4:15). Paul wrote, "But God demonstrates his own love for us in this: While we were still sinners, Christ died for us" (Romans 5:8).

4. What images come to mind when you think of love?

5. Is it possible for something impersonal to love or be loved? Why or why not?

6. What differences do you see in the two kinds of gods portrayed by the statements above?

NEW AGE GOD	BIBLICAL GOD

Will the Real Judge Please Stand?

Dr. Bernie Siegel is a surgeon, the president of the American Holistic Medical Association, the author of *Love, Medicine & Miracles,* and a strong believer in the ability of the patient to heal himself. He's very popular among New Agers. In an interview, Siegel expressed his opinions about the afterlife: "If you say to me, do I believe we live on in some other kind of energy after the body dies, yes. . . . But whether it goes to heaven or just goes back to the original source of energy that created the universe, if you want to call it God—I mean, you are just playing games with words—what's the difference? And can that energy pick out a new body? I don't know. I mean, what difference does it make?"[6]

7. What difference do you think it would make to have an afterlife with an impersonal energy or a personal Being? (You might look at John 14:2-3 and Revelation 21:1-3.)

AFTERLIFE WITH AN IMPERSONAL ENERGY WOULD BE LIKE THIS	AFTERLIFE WITH A PERSONAL BEING WOULD BE LIKE THIS

8. In these two kinds of afterlife, which God is more judgmental? Why?

9. Most New Agers believe in reincarnation, which asserts
that a person's spirit is born into another body, lifetime
after lifetime. Your new life is better or worse, depending
upon the *karma*—your past actions, whether good or
bad—that you built up during your former life.

   Others see death as a natural step along a journey
through innumerable spiritual levels on the way to the
goal of perfection and mastery. Death is not a form of
judgment, they say, and it is certainly not something to
be feared. Contrast the assurances a New Ager has when
facing death with the assurances that a Christian has (see
John 14:1-3, 1 Corinthians 15:54-57, 2 Corinthians 5:1-5,
Philippians 1:23).

NEW AGE ASSURANCES	CHRISTIAN ASSURANCES

To close, take a few moments to thank God for being the
kind of Person the Bible says He is: an intimately loving and
morally responsive Father. Thank Him for justly and lovingly
dealing with the consequences of your moral choices so you
have no reason to fear death. Also, keep praying for your
New Age friends and neighbors.

NOTES
1. We will define a *person* as a living being who has intelligence (is rational,
wise, self-aware, with a center of consciousness), emotions (love, anger, joy,
and so on), volition (purposefulness), and moral sensitivities.
2. Marilyn Ferguson, *The Aquarian Conspiracy: Personal and Social Transformation in the 1980s* (Los Angeles, CA: J. P. Tarcher, 1980), page 382.

3. Stuart Wilde, *The Force* (Taos, NM: White Dove International, 1984), page 55.
4. Wilde, page 10 (italics added).
5. Shirley MacLaine, *Out on a Limb* (New York: Bantam Books, 1983), page 202 (italics added).
6. Florence Graves, "The High Priest of Healing," *New Age Journal* (May/June 1989), page 92.

CHANNELERS AND SPIRIT-GUIDES

Warm-up
What difference would it make to you if you could not personally talk with God?

Why Channeling?
What is channeling? Researchers of channeling have not arrived at a consensus concerning that question. The source of the controversy lies primarily in what is being channeled. Some say the information being channeled is derived from a vast sea of mind that is common to every person and available through intuition. Others say the source of information is probably a personalized, disembodied entity and receiving information from it is more a matter of communication from one being to another than intuition. Still others contend that channeling is merely a psychological phenomenon that has nothing to do with the supernatural.

Channeling did not play a prominent part in the beginnings of the New Age movement during the 1960s and early 1970s, but it was around. Some New Agers consulted the older works of Edgar Cayce, who died in 1945. But there were more recent examples of channeling, such as the "Seth" material of Jane Roberts and the channeling experiences of David Spangler and the Caddy family at Findhorn, Scotland.

In the 1980s, channeling has come to play a more central role in the New Age movement. Shirley MacLaine's ABC miniseries, "Out on a Limb," assisted in that process by featuring channeler Kevin Ryerson. There were also others who contributed to channeling's increasing popularity, the most famous of whom were J. Z. Knight, who channels Ramtha, and Jach Pursel, who channels Lazaris.

Today the trend is going beyond depending on others to act as intermediaries between the spiritual seeker and the higher spiritual beings. Now New Agers are being encouraged to personally contact their own spirit-guides.

1. As we saw in the last chapter, the god of the New Age is abstract, impersonal, and distant, in that it is unaware of our suffering. In light of such a god, why do you suppose channeling and contacting one's spirit-guide has become popular among New Agers? What void does it fill?

Why Does the Bible Prohibit Spiritism?
As Christians, we are aware that the Bible prohibits spiritistic activity (Leviticus 19:31, 20:6; Deuteronomy 18:10-11; 1 Chronicles 10:13; Isaiah 8:19), but the reasons why might not be clear. In the following questions, we will explore why spiritism is prohibited in the Bible.

2. In the Garden of Eden, the serpent tempted Eve by saying, "You will not surely die. . . . For God knows that when you eat of it your eyes will be opened, and you will be like God, knowing good and evil" (Genesis 3:4-5). How do those words resemble New Age teachings?

3. Some New Agers acknowledge that "negative" spirits exist, but they assume they have the innate ability to discern between the "negative" and the good spirits. But what factor mentioned in John 8:44 and 2 Corinthians

11:14 complicates such a natural ability for discernment? Why?

4. Look at Genesis 3:1-6. How is the serpent's method of
temptation in the garden consistent with 2 Corinthians
11:14?

After extensively researching channeling, Jon Klimo, writing from a pro-channeling position, described the common
themes that are coming out of these channeled messages:

> Virtually all of the sources above the lower astral levels
> tell us that from their vantage points they know the
> entire universe to be a living spiritual Being of which
> each is a living part. According to Universal Law, we
> are evolving through a series of embodied and disem-
> bodied lives toward an eventual reunion with the one
> God, which is the underlying identity of All That Is.
> In the meantime, we maintain an ongoing condition of
> identity with this God, though we are unaware of it.[1]

5. Judging by Klimo's assessment, in what ways do channeled teachings oppose Christian theology?

6. In light of what you've been discussing, why do you
think the Bible commands us not to contact the spirits?

The Holy Spirit
As Christians, we have the Holy Spirit to offer in place of the
channeled messages and spirit-guides of the New Age. The
Holy Spirit, moreover, is not merely on a "higher" spiritual
plane, but is God Himself (Acts 5:3,5). Through the Holy
Spirit, we can be in direct fellowship with God.

The Holy Spirit does not initially bring a message that is pleasant, though, for Jesus said, "When he [the Holy Spirit] comes, he will convict the world of guilt in regard to sin and righteousness and judgment" (John 16:8). That's the bad news. But there is good news that has to do with the indwelling of the Holy Spirit. Read Paul's words concerning this indwelling:

> [God] anointed us, set his seal of ownership on us, and put his Spirit in our hearts as a deposit, guaranteeing what is to come. (2 Corinthians 1:21-22)

> Therefore, if anyone is in Christ, he is a new creation. (2 Corinthians 5:17)

> Having believed [in Jesus], you were marked in him with a seal, the promised Holy Spirit, who is a deposit guaranteeing our inheritance until the redemption of those who are God's possession. (Ephesians 1:13-14)

Consider also Jesus' words: "But the Counselor, the Holy Spirit, whom the Father will send in my name, will teach you all things and will remind you of everything I have said to you" (John 14:26).

7. Contrast what the Holy Spirit guarantees with what the channeled spirits guarantee, according to Klimo's summary.

HOLY SPIRIT	CHANNELED SPIRITS

8. In light of this discussion on the Holy Spirit, what does the Christian gospel have to offer to the New Ager who is seeking the wisdom of channelers or spirit-guides?

Have someone pray and thank God for the Holy Spirit, especially for the fact that He indwells us, transforms us, and guarantees our place with God in eternity.

NOTE
1. Jon Klimo, *Channeling* (New York: J. P. Tarcher, 1987), page 150.

NEW AGE HEALING

Warm-up

Have you ever prayed that God would heal someone and the person wasn't healed? If so, how did you feel?

In Maine, around 1840, doctors informed Phinehas Quimby that he was terminally ill with tuberculosis. As a kind of psychic second opinion, Lucius Burkmar, Quimby's friend, looked at the condition of Quimby's lungs and kidneys through clairvoyance and confirmed what the doctors had said. Burkmar went further than the doctors, though: He convinced Quimby that he could be healed. Soon, Quimby was healed, attributing his healing to the power of the mind.

He wrote that whereas the doctors had "deceived [me] into a belief that made me sick . . . [Burkmar's] ideas were so absurd that the disease vanished by the absurdity of the cure."[1] As a result of his experience, Quimby devoted his life to helping others discover the power of the mind to heal. From Quimby's ideas grew Christian Science and the New Thought movement, which includes the Unity School of Christianity and the Church of Religious Science.

The New Thought movement was one of the movements that contributed to the New Age movement. The influence of New Thought on the New Age can be seen in its emphasis on the healing powers of the mind. Listen to the words of Shakti Gawain, a popular New Age speaker and author: "Our bodies are simply a physical expression of our consciousness.

The concepts we hold of ourselves determine our health and beauty or the lack thereof. When we deeply change our concepts, our physical self follows suit."[2]

1. What do you think about the idea that the body directly reflects the condition of the mind and that the mind can heal the body? Which statements would you agree with?

   a. Emotional stress can cause headaches.
   b. An unforgiving spirit can cause cancer.
   c. You can kill cancer cells by visualizing (forming a mental picture of) the healthy cells killing the unhealthy ones.
   d. Laughter will cure terminal heart disease.
   e. The mind has the power to heal a broken leg.
   f. The body has an energy force flowing through and around it.
   g. When the body's energy force is out of balance, illness results.
   h. The mind either channels or blocks our natural healing forces, depending on our attitude.
   i. By examining the colors of the iris in an eye, an iridologist can tell what is wrong with the body.

The Spirit in Holistic Health

The Bible speaks of a person's attitude, or mind, as being a factor in his or her health: "A cheerful heart is good medicine, but a crushed spirit dries up the bones" (Proverbs 17:22). In that respect, then, Christians could agree with New Agers concerning the influence of the mind on the body. David uses similar words when talking about the physical effects of his sin: "My bones have no soundness because of my sin. My guilt has overwhelmed me like a burden too heavy to bear. My wounds fester and are loathsome because of my sinful folly" (Psalm 38:3-5).

The theory of holistic health is that the mind, body, and spirit must all be taken into consideration before the cause of an illness and its cure can be found. While such a theory has validity, many in the holistic health movement define *spirit* as a form of ultimate universal energy. In other words, they are talking about their concept of ultimate reality, or God. For example, the editors of the *New Age Journal* said:

> All of the healing systems that can be called "holistic" share a common belief in the universe as a unified field of energy that produces all form and substance. . . . This vital force, which supports and sustains life, has been given many names. The Chinese call it "chi'i," the Hindus call it "prana," the Hebrews call it "ruach," and the American Indians name it "the Great Spirit. . . ." Some people call this power-that-connects, love, or divine energy.[3]

2. According to the above quote, what kind of religious perspective is being promoted by many in holistic health?

3. David says spiritual problems like sin (crossing a personal God's moral boundaries) have physical effects. Would a New Ager agree? Why or why not?

4. (Optional) The Hebrew word *ruach* means "breath," "wind," or "spirit," whether God's or man's. Read Genesis 1:2, 2:7, 7:15; Job 33:4; and Isaiah 11:1-4. How is the biblical idea of spirit like and unlike that given in the *New Age Journal*?

The Object of Faith

Typically, those who talk about the healing powers of the mind use language that implies guarantees. Shakti Gawain says, "The more we bring our consciousness into alignment with our highest spiritual realization, the more our bodies will express our own individual perfection."[4] Gawain is claiming that there is a direct cause-and-effect relationship between the state of a person's mind and his physical condition.

Jesus also talked about healing in a way that implied guarantees. He said to the two blind men, "According to your faith will it be done to you" (Matthew 9:29), and to the sick woman, "your faith has healed you" (Matthew 9:22).

5. Was Jesus Christ saying the same thing as Shakti Gawain? Explain.

6. What about those who are not healed? According to the New Age perspective, where would the problem be?

7. How would a Christian approach a similar situation of not being healed?

8. When is the Christian assured of being healed?

9. When is the New Ager assured of being healed?

The Purpose of Healing

To say that God doesn't *always* heal today is not to say that He never heals. Sometimes He heals miraculously, for a variety of purposes. Some of those purposes are expressed in the words of Peter after he had healed a crippled man:

> "Why do you stare at us as if by our own power or godliness we had made this man walk? The God of Abraham, Isaac and Jacob, the God of our fathers, has glorified his servant Jesus. . . . By faith in the name of Jesus, this man whom you see and know was made strong. . . . Repent, then, and turn to God, so that your sins may be wiped out." (Acts 3:12-13,16,19)

10. What, according to Peter, are some of the purposes of miraculous healing?

11. What part of the above verses is particularly relevant as a critique of the New Age approach to healing?

Thank God that He does glorify Jesus—not our power or godliness—by healing people. If you or anyone you know is ill, this might be a good time to pray for their healing. Pray especially for sick New Agers you know, that God would seize a chance to bring them to the end of their trust in themselves and reveal Himself as a powerful and loving personal Savior-Healer.

NOTES
1. H. W. Dresser, *A History of the New Thought Movement* (London: George G. Harrap, n.d.), pages 33-34.
2. Shakti Gawain, *Creative Visualization* (New York: Bantam Books, 1985), page 59.
3. Rick Fields, et al., eds., *Chop Wood, Carry Water* (Los Angeles, CA: J. P. Tarcher, 1984), page 186.
4. Gawain, page 59.

WHAT'S THE BIG DEAL ABOUT SIN?

Warm-up

If someone slanders you publicly, then tells you that he doesn't feel at all guilty about his actions because he starts each day with a clean slate, how would you feel? What would you do?

New Agers place a lot of emphasis on the power of the mind, finding hope in the idea that as we change our self-image, we can transform ourselves and the world. For example, Jonathan Parker, the founder of Gateways Institute, has said, "It may come as a surprise, but how you feel about yourself in the deepest part of your being—*your self-image—is the greatest force in your life.* . . . You *can* change your self-image, and in doing so, start building a life of happiness, radiant health, and good fortune."[1]

Gateways Institute attempts to help people change their self-image through subliminal suggestion. It offers tapes designed in such a way that on the conscious level you hear either music or nature sounds, but on the subconscious level you hear words of affirmation. The following subliminal affirmations are recorded on a Gateways' tape entitled "Releasing Guilts": "I forgive and release myself of all guilt. There is a sense of peace and tranquility about me. I hold only positive, loving thoughts and memories. I am free of condemnation and guilt. It is dissolved and gone. I start each day with a clean slate."[2]

1. What if you listened to the "Releasing Guilts" tape and believe you are forgiven and released from all guilt, by whom and on what basis have you been forgiven?

2. Why is such a method of dealing with guilt incompatible with Christian teaching? What specific factors are missing? Consider the following verses:

   When I kept silent, my bones wasted away through my groaning all day long. . . . Then I acknowledged my sin to you and did not cover up my iniquity. I said, "I will confess my transgressions to the LORD"—and you forgave the guilt of my sin. (Psalm 32:3,5)

   "Holy, holy, holy is the LORD Almighty." (Isaiah 6:3)

The Problem of Guilt
New Agers believe the problem of guilt doesn't go beyond our minds because the god of the New Age is a nonmoral force, an impersonal oneness without moral distinctions. Moral terms such as right and wrong simply do not apply to an impersonal force, any more than we hold a hurricane morally responsible for its actions. Moral issues are not involved when relating to an impersonal force. Lying and stealing are irrelevant for relating to electrical energy, and the same is true of the New Age god.

If God is personal, though, moral terms do apply. This can be illustrated through everyday human relationships, where moral issues such as respect, trust, and honesty are important. Take the relationship between you and the clerk at the grocery store. If you are rude to him, he won't be enthusiastic about serving you, and if he cheats you, you won't think very well of him.

Of course, if God is personal, then sin is real. When we

sin, we rebel against God's moral character and authority, which alienates us from God, and this alienation is just as real as the alienation that results from slandering a friend.

The Apostle John wrote, "If we claim to be without sin, we deceive ourselves and the truth is not in us. If we confess our sins, he is faithful and just and will forgive us our sins and purify us from all unrighteousness" (1 John 1:8–9).

3. While the bad news of God being personal is that sin is real, what does John say is the good news?

4. The good news of a god being impersonal is that sin does not alienate us from that god because all that exists comes from the ultimate oneness. But what would the bad news be about forgiveness? Consider the following thoughts of Shirley MacLaine and her friend David.

David said, "It all comes back to the individual, the person. Shirley, *that's* what karma means. Whatever action one takes will ultimately return to that person—good and bad—maybe not in this life embodiment, but sometime in the future. And no one is exempt."[3]

Later, MacLaine reflected, "For every act, for every indifference, for every misuse of life, we are finally held accountable. And it is up to us to understand what those accounts might be."[4]

What's So Bad About Sin?

Unless a person is aware that he or she has sinned against God, the message of the cross will seem like foolishness. How do we as Christians approach the subject of sin with a New Ager? For starters, we can only point to its reality. It is beyond our ability to convict them of sin, since the Holy Spirit is the only One who can work in a person's heart.

One thing that New Agers really have a hard time understanding is why the God of the Bible gets so upset about sin. Sure, we break His law, but why can't He just forgive and forget? After all, most parents are able to forgive their children for their disobedience. New Agers wonder how humans could be more forgiving and loving than God.

What is it about sin that causes such an irreparable break between us and God? What is so bad is the attitude involved when we sin. Jesus said, "For out of the heart come evil thoughts, murder, adultery, sexual immorality, theft, false testimony, slander. These are what make a man 'unclean'" (Matthew 15:19).

Paul makes the same connection between our attitude and our sinful behavior: "Once you were alienated from God and were enemies in your minds because of your evil behavior" (Colossians 1:21). Sin is rooted in the attitude of saying to God, "I reject Your authority to tell me what is right and wrong. I have the right to choose the standard by which I will live. I am the master of my fate, accountable to no one but myself." If that's the attitude we have in our hearts, it's understandable why our relationship with God is broken.

5. Does the above assessment of the attitude behind sin overstate the case or match what you have experienced about sin?

6. One way of pointing to our self-centered attitude toward God is to show how that same attitude shows up in the way we relate to our family, friends, coworkers, the environment, and international relations. Give some examples of how it is revealed.

7. Some New Agers will say that their lives are more moral than that of some Christians. While a moral life

is all right as far as it goes, why isn't it enough? What kind of change is God looking for? Consider the following verses:

The sacrifices of God are a broken spirit; a broken and contrite heart, O God, you will not despise. (Psalm 51:17)

He has showed you, O man, what is good. And what does the LORD require of you? To act justly and to love mercy and to walk humbly with your God. (Micah 6:8)

"Blessed are the poor in spirit,
    for theirs is the kingdom of heaven. . . .
Blessed are those who hunger and thirst for
        righteousness,
    for they will be filled." (Matthew 5:3,6)

8. For the New Ager, the first step on a person's spiritual trek is to realize his inner perfection. For the Christian, the first step is to realize his fallenness before God. The New Ager deals with his guilt before God by denying it; the Christian, by confessing it. According to your experience, what is the emotional effect of denying your guilt to God or to someone you have wronged?

9. What is the emotional and relational effect of confessing your guilt to God or another person?

What can you find in this session to thank God for? Take about five minutes to do this. Have each person in the group offer one sentence of thanks.

NOTES
1. Jonathan Parker, *Gateways to Self-Discovery* (Ojai, CA: Gateways Institute, n.d.), page 6.
2. Parker, page 28.
3. Shirley MacLaine, *Out on a Limb* (New York: Bantam Books, 1983), page 96.
4. MacLaine, page 111.

GOD LOVES YOU, BUT . . .

One thing New Agers and Christians agree upon: God is love. But what does that mean? Anuradha Vittachi tells the story of a conversation he had with Mother Teresa:

> I asked her my question. Do we not need to learn to love ourselves, to learn that we are loveable, before we can love others? It is a difficult process for many of us.
>
> She seemed surprised that valuing myself was a problem. She replied with simple certainty. "But you are precious to God."
>
> Something happened for me in that moment. It was as if the walls fell open. I was overwhelmed by a feeling of being loved, of being indeed valuable, precious to life itself. . . . Of course, I wanted to say; how could I have been so stupid? It was as though I had been searching everywhere with my head down, when I only needed to look up.[1]

1. Can you relate to Mr. Vittachi's experience? How did it affect your life when you first realized that God loves you?

God Is Light, and God Is Love

While it can be a transforming experience to realize that
God loves us, this love must be based in truth. Many New
Agers presume upon God's love. To them it is a given;
they believe God can do nothing but love. The story
of Marcie, who went through a near-death experience
(NDE), illustrates this presumption.

During Marcie's NDE she felt herself in the presence
of "an incredibly warm, indescribably brilliant light." She
said the light was "totally loving and safe," interconnecting
all things: "You are the light and it is you, and it is connected
at once to everything else in the universe. The light is conscious and intelligent, and in it you share that intelligence.
Suddenly everything that has happened in your life makes
complete sense."

As a result of her NDE, Marcie says she has come to
realize that "the only lesson we're here to learn is the lesson
of love. Suddenly the worn-out phrase 'God is love' was
totally clear. . . . Since that time, I have lost my fear of death.
I just don't believe in it anymore."[2]

2. a. What is your immediate response to the loving light
that Marcie encountered?

   b. We don't know much about Marcie, but we can safely
   assume that she is not a notoriously evil person. But
   what if she were? What if you were to replace the
   character of Marcie in this NDE with a habitual rapist,
   or a man who had just gunned down twenty children
   while they played in their school playground? What if
   this person, moreover, refused to learn the lesson of
   love, but enjoyed wreaking havoc in other people's
   lives, and continued to do so no matter how many
   times he encountered the loving light?

3. What do you think of this divine light that accepts all people into its presence with undiscriminating love? Would you consider such a god just or holy? Someone you respect? Why or why not?

4. John writes in his gospel, "This is the verdict: Light has come into the world, but men loved darkness instead of light because their deeds were evil" (John 3:19). Who is John's light? How does this Light differ from the light in Marcie's NDE?

Marcie says her experience taught her what the phrase "God is love" means. There is no question that God's love is needed today. However, consider its biblical meaning:

> God is love. This is how God showed his love among us: He sent his one and only Son into the world that we might live through him. This is love: not that we loved God, but that he loved us and sent his Son as an atoning sacrifice for our sins. (1 John 4:8-10)

According to John, God demonstrated His love through the historical incarnation of Jesus Christ, and for a specific purpose.

5. a. What was that purpose? Why did God send Jesus? (Try to explain in simple terms.)

   b. How does that distinguish the biblical meaning of "God is love" from Marcie's meaning?

The Dilemma Presented by Evil

The fact that there is evil in us (we often don't do the things we know we should and do the things we know we shouldn't) presents God with a dilemma: What is He to do with us? If God is holy and just, then He cannot accept us as we are, for that would mean He condones our sin. But if God is loving, then neither would He destroy us. How, then, are we to be reconciled to God? How are we to become acceptable in His sight?

6. Judging by the loving light that Marcie encountered, how does the god of the New Age deal with this dilemma?

7. Judging by 2 Corinthians 5:21 and 1 John 4:8-10, how does the Bible say God dealt with this dilemma?

A Searching Love

The Dalai Lama, spiritual leader for the Tibetan Buddhists, once said, "Lovingkindness is the universal religion. In order to develop [a] healthy human society, [we] need more harmony."[3] How could anyone possibly disagree with such words? After all, no one would contend that the world has an over-abundance of love and harmony.

In 1 John 4:8-10, though, there is the distinct sense that God's love is not to be confused with just any love. Instead, God's love was specifically demonstrated through a particular Person at a certain time for a definite purpose, which was to deal with humanity's sin nature.

God's love, then, is not about peace and harmony, but about a blinding light that exposes the spiritual darkness within. "Everyone who does evil hates the light, and will not come into the light for fear that his deeds will be exposed" (John 3:20). God's love doesn't initially soothe; instead, it searches into the depths of your being. Then it acts like a

surgical knife to cut out the sickness before the healing transformation can begin.

8. a. The Dalai Lama's words are appealing, but to what
part of us do they appeal?

b. What does he assume about humanity?

c. Where is he encouraging us to place our hope?

9. How would you summarize the differences between the
New Age god and the Christian God that you have discussed in this session?

10. What difference does this contrast make to you personally?

This has been a somewhat difficult chapter to work through.
Take some time to pray and thank God for the tough love that
He has given us through Jesus Christ.

NOTES
1. Anuradha Vittachi, *Earth Conference One* (Boston: Shambhala, 1989),
page 69.
2. Joan Borysenko, "Spiritual ReVision: Moving from Guilt to Grace," *New Age
Journal,* April 1990, page 32.
3. Vittachi, page 73.

OPEN-MINDEDNESS AND THE WAY TO GOD

One of the most frustrating attitudes that a Christian can encounter when attempting to share Christ with a New Ager is the attitude that truth is relative. According to the New Age movement, the only absolute truth is that no truth is absolute; truth depends on the perspective of the individual. Such relativity can be frustrating because no matter how good a case you might make for Christianity, the New Ager can always respond, "Well, that might be true for you, but it's not true for me." New Agers consider it taboo for any religion to claim that only it is true.

An attitude that closely accompanies that of relativity is open-mindedness. New Agers assert that all spiritual paths are acceptable and no single path is better than another. They say that whichever path suits you best is the one you should travel.

1. Share an experience where you encountered open-mindedness and/or relativity.

2. Belief systems always make claims about truth. The problem is that the New Age movement and Christianity make contradictory claims, and both cannot be right. Based on what you know about the New Age movement and Christianity, list some ways they contradict each other . . .

a. With respect to God:

NEW AGE	CHRISTIANITY
God is . . .	God is . . .

b. With respect to humanity:

NEW AGE	CHRISTIANITY
Humanity is . . .	Humanity is . . .

c. With respect to life after death:

NEW AGE	CHRISTIANITY
Life after death is . . .	Life after death is . . .

3. How would Scripture view the attitudes of open-mindedness and relativity toward the way of salvation? (See Matthew 7:13-14, John 14:6, Acts 4:12.)

The Way to God: Many or One?

When it comes to open-mindedness and relativity, God's personhood is relevant. If, as the New Agers teach, God is an impersonal oneness without distinctions, it is understandable why they say truth is relative. If God is personal, though, truth can't be relative. Like any other person, certain things are true about Him and certain things are false. Either God created all things, or He did not. Either God is separate from His creation, or He is not. Either God is morally holy, or He is not. Either Jesus is the unique Son of God, or He is not.

Concerning whether there are many ways or only one way of salvation, it's important to understand why "small is the gate and narrow the road that leads to life" (Matthew 7:14). As far as there being one or many ways to salvation, there are as many ways to God as there are ways to receive forgiveness from a person you have wronged.

Jesus' parable of the prodigal son perfectly illustrates why the way of salvation is exclusive (see Luke 15:11-32). The son didn't just leave his father, he rejected him—and everything about him. He rejected his father's physical presence ("set off for a distant country"), his financial wisdom ("squandered his wealth"), and his moral standards ("wild living").

4. Read Luke 15:11-32. When and how did the son decide to return to his father?

5. Discuss how the parable, coupled with the statement that "there are as many ways to God as there are ways to receive forgiveness from a person you have wronged," illustrate Matthew 7:14, "small is the gate and narrow the road that leads to life."

Salvation as a Path

At one New Age fair, a sign hung on the entrance doors, proclaiming, "All world religions are paths to God and Love."

Notice where such a statement places the emphasis concerning how to reach God: on the *path* that *we* must travel. New Age salvation is a path we must walk in order to reach God; it is not God reaching out to us. The New Age way of salvation is based on human effort, not on God's grace.

NEW AGE	CHRISTIANITY
Good news: Many paths to God.	*Bad news:* One way to God.
Bad news: Salvation is based on human effort.	*Good news:* Salvation is based on God's grace.

The following chart elaborates on the contrasting ways of salvation.

NEW AGE SALVATION . . .	BIBLICAL SALVATION . . .
1. Means merging with the impersonal oneness.	1. Means being reconciled with the Person of God.
2. Is based on human effort.	2. Is based on God's grace.
3. Points to Jesus as an example of what a self-actualized person is like.	3. Points to Jesus as our substitute for the death penalty for our sin, and our example of what a person living by God's power is like.
4. Points to some standard of perfection that must be met in order to achieve salvation.	4. Points to humanity's sinfulness, which means we cannot possibly merit salvation.
5. Is a gradual process in order to manifest perfection.	5. Is an immediate gift that can be received by faith in Jesus Christ.

6. Which aspects of the above chart appear in the following statements?

Shirley MacLaine: "[Reincarnation] is like show business. You keep doing it until you get it right."[1]

The Unity School of Christianity: "The mere 'shedding of blood' on the cross was not to relieve man from the necessity of achieving his own dominion and mastery. Jesus Christ was not meant to be slain as a substitute for man; that is, to atone vicariously for him. Each person must achieve at-one-ment with God, by letting the Christ Spirit within him resurrect his soul into Christ perfection."[2]

7. a. How would you feel if you knew the New Age system were true?

   b. What would you do differently?

8. In light of what you have discussed throughout this session, how could you explain to a friend that the Christian view of salvation is better news than the New Age view?

Thank God for salvation by grace through faith in Jesus Christ. Tell Him what has struck you most about that truth today.

NOTES
1. Shirley MacLaine, *Out on a Limb* (New York: Bantam, 1983), page 233.
2. *The Way to Salvation* (Unity Village, MO: Unity, 1973), page 6.

THE UNIQUENESS OF JESUS

Jesus once asked His disciples, "Who do the crowds say I am?" After they gave a range of answers, Jesus then asked, "But what about you?" Peter answered, "The Christ of God" (Luke 9:18-20). Jesus considered it important that people understood who He was.

While New Agers acknowledge Jesus as the Christ, they do so in such a way that they deny His uniqueness. To them, the Christ is the principle of divinity or perfection that lies within each person. In our true selves, we are each the Christ. They assert that the only thing unique about Jesus was that He was one of the very few people in history who fully realized and manifested their Christhood. As such, New Agers see Jesus as our supreme example, the One who demonstrated the unlimited power that we all have the potential to manifest.

The gospels paint an entirely different picture. In them, the Christ is not a principle shared by everyone, but a Person who was the unique fulfillment of Old Testament prophecy and uniquely related to God. It is clear that John the Baptist was fully aware of the uniqueness of the Christ when he refused to accept that title (see John 1:20). Moreover, the Apostle John wrote his gospel so people "may believe that *Jesus is the Christ, the Son of God,* and that by believing you may have life in his name" (John 20:31, italics added).

In two different conversations—one with Peter and another with Martha—Jesus makes His identity as the Christ the primary issue of faith (see Matthew 16:13-20, John 11:25-27). Significantly, when they acknowledged Him as the Christ, He did not reciprocate by saying, "You, too, have the Christ principle within." He did warn that others would come and falsely claim to be the Christ (Matthew 24:4-5,23-24).

After being arrested, Jesus stood before the high priest, who demanded, "Tell us if you are the Christ, the Son of God." Since the penalty for a wrong answer was death, it would have been a convenient time for Jesus to deny being the Christ or to water down its offense to the Jews by saying that everyone had the Christ principle within them. Nevertheless, Jesus answered, "Yes, it is as you say" (Matthew 26:63-64). For giving that answer, He paid with His life.

The issue of the Christ illustrates a common tactic that New Agers take with respect to Jesus: denying His uniqueness.

1. Why is it important to the New Age movement to deny that Jesus is unique?

2. Why is the uniqueness of Jesus important to Christianity?

3. Besides being uniquely the Christ, what are some other ways Jesus is unique? Read the following verses.

    a. John 1:1-3, 5:18; 1 Corinthians 8:6; Philippians 2:6; Colossians 1:15-20; Hebrews 1:1-3

    b. Luke 1:32-33,35; John 3:16

c. Luke 23:40-41, John 8:46, 2 Corinthians 5:21, Hebrews 4:15, 1 John 3:5

d. John 1:29; Acts 4:12; Titus 2:13 (compare with 3:4,6); Hebrews 9:28

What If . . .

Many New Agers are not attracted to Christianity because they don't see its relevance. Why, they ask, do Christians spend so much time talking about a Person who lived two thousand years ago? What relevance does He have for us today? New Agers are looking for answers that work now.

4. Suppose someone today predicted not only how, when, where, and at whose hands he or she was going to die, but also predicted that he or she would physically rise from the dead three days later. Then suppose that this person's predictions came true. Would you feel that such an event might be relevant for your life? Why?

5. What questions would you want to ask this person?

The Relevance of the Resurrection

Of course, the situation posed in the previous section is precisely what happened to Jesus. He predicted the details of His death and resurrection:

> Now as Jesus was going up to Jerusalem, he took the twelve disciples aside and said to them, "We are going up to Jerusalem, and the Son of Man will be betrayed to the chief priests and the teachers of the law. They will condemn him to death and will turn him over to the

Gentiles to be mocked and flogged and crucified. On the third day he will be raised to life!" (Matthew 20:17-19; see also Matthew 12:40; 16:4,21; 17:22-23; 26:2)

What is most amazing is that His predictions came true! The following questions will show you why Jesus' death and resurrection are relevant for us today.

The Past

6. Jesus made some amazing claims about Himself. He claimed that He existed with God in eternity (John 17:5); that He was the "I am" (John 8:58; compare with Exodus 3:14); that God had committed all judgment to Him (John 5:22); that God was His Father, and They were One (John 10:30); that He had the authority to forgive sins on God's behalf (Matthew 9:4-6); that anyone who had known and seen Jesus had known and seen God the Father (John 8:19, 14:9); and that He was the only way to the Father (John 14:6). What bearing does Jesus' resurrection have on the credibility of His claims?

7. Have one person look up each of the following verses and think about what they mean. Then discuss the meaning and significance of what Jesus accomplished on the cross: Romans 3:21-26, 4:23-25, 8:1; Ephesians 1:7; Colossians 1:19-22; 1 John 4:10.

The Present

8. Read Romans 6:5-14 and 8:9-16. Then discuss how Jesus' resurrection is relevant for us today.

The Future

9. How will Christ Jesus' resurrection be relevant for us
   in the future? Read Romans 8:23 and 1 Corinthians
   15:20-22,50-57.

How Do We Know It Is True?

The primary source for learning about Jesus' life, teachings,
death, and resurrection is the New Testament. But how do
we know we can trust it? New Agers believe the Bible is the
fallible word of men, not the inspired Word of God.

While a detailed defense of the New Testament is
beyond the scope of this session, one thing can be said:
The resurrection of Jesus explains the transformation of the
disciples better than anything else. After Jesus' arrest, the disciples' hopes were dashed. The One they had thought was the
Messiah was about to be crucified. They distanced themselves
from Jesus, and most of them hid in a locked room. Peter
even denied that he was one of Jesus' followers.

Within a few days, though, these same men began to
boldly proclaim that Jesus had risen from the dead. Because
they were living in a Jewish culture where blasphemy was
punishable by death, the disciples had nothing to gain and
everything to lose by forming a religion that worshiped
Jesus. Indeed, all but one of them paid with their lives for
proclaiming that Jesus was the risen Lord and Savior. People
do not voluntarily die for a lie.

What changed these men? The only adequate explanation is that Jesus actually rose from the dead. No other
explanation supplies the power that was needed to thrust the
Church into existence.

While it's important to have confidence in the historical
accuracy of the Bible, what will make the biggest impression
on a New Ager is the life lived by a Christian friend. Because
Jesus Christ is unique, the way of following Christ is unique.
It is unique because its central message is not that of a path
or a religion, but a Person and a relationship. We speak of the

religion of Christianity, but in truth our goal is not to convert people to a religion, but to help them know and love a Person—Jesus Christ, the Son of God.

10. In light of the uniqueness of life in Christ, what must be true of our own lives before we can effectively introduce others to Jesus Christ?

Have several in the class pray that we will be effective witnesses for Jesus Christ to those in the New Age movement and that the Church will mobilize to reach this segment of society that is searching but is lost.

LEADER'S GUIDE

This section includes background information and suggestions for leading a group discussion.

WHAT IS THE NEW AGE?

Goals
1. To define the New Age.
2. To provide guidelines for detecting the influence of the New Age.
3. To provide a case study on how to approach the problem of New Age influence in public schools.

Reading Aloud
You may decide whether to let group members read the information sections silently or to have one or more people read a section aloud while the group follows along. Perhaps the best approach is to alternate for variety.

Warm-up
The purpose of a warm-up question is to break the ice and let you know where group members are coming from as you begin a study. In this warm-up, you're looking for the impressions and stereotypes group members are carrying around with them. Explain that you are not asking for a balanced, carefully reasoned response, but just one sentence describing a picture or idea they have of the New Age movement. For instance: "To me, the term *New Age* brings to mind Shirley MacLaine standing on the beach shouting, 'I am god!'" Kind

humor is great in a warm-up, but keep the discussion moving, because this isn't the meat of the session.

Transformation is the primary purpose of the training that Werner Erhard developed: "The *est* training seeks to create the condition under which individual transformation can occur."[1] In light of the attitude common among New Agers that we are able to transform ourselves, I am reminded of a comic strip in which a man was obviously drowning. Both hands were raised in desperation, and the man was yelling, "Self-help! Self-help!"

Ways to Detect New Age Influence

About humanity's perfection, John P. Hanley, Lifespring's founder, said, "We are perfect exactly the way we are. And when we accept that, life works."[2] Discussing the unlimited nature of humanity's potential and knowledge, a Lifespring brochure stated, "[Lifespring] views people as having unlimited potential and knowledge within them."[3] As for our having the power to determine and shape reality, Hanley himself said, "I am 100 percent responsible for whatever happens in my life."[4]

One person who experienced the Lifespring training reported that the trainer said, "You are accountable for everything that happens to you, from the moment you pick your own parents till you choose the moment of your death."[5] As bizarre as that might sound, it's a common belief among New Agers. For example, Dr. Norbert Glass, a follower of Rudolf Steiner, wrote in *Conception, Birth, and Early Childhood* that each person exists before he is born and that he or she, while "striving for incarnation, chooses his parents."[6]

This New Age tendency to attribute to humanity the powers of God can also be seen in a statement made in an interview by the late Beverly Gaylean, who developed a program called Confluent Education for the Los Angeles Public Schools:

> Once we begin to see that we are all God, that we all have the attributes of God, then I think the whole purpose of human life is to reown the Godlikeness within

us; the perfect love, the perfect wisdom, the perfect understanding, the perfect intelligence, and when we do that, we create back to that old, that essential oneness which is consciousness.[7]

The New Age movement gives respectability to the idea that we possess the power to create our own reality through its interpretation of quantum mechanics, the study of the sub-atomic realm. New Agers say that quantum mechanics shows that an infinite number of possible universes exist in a potential realm. By our act of observation, we bring one particular universe into actuality. Marilyn Ferguson, for example, suggests that "Our brains mathematically construct 'hard' reality by interpreting frequencies from a dimension transcending time and space."[8] Michael Talbot wrote that "All possible realities coexist" and that "the consciousness contains a 'reality structurer,' some neurophysiological mechanism which psychically affects reality itself."[9] Finally, Gary Zukav wrote, "*Who is looking at the universe?* Put another way, *How is the universe being actualized?* The answer comes full circle. *We* are actualizing the universe."[10]

Question 5
People are attracted to the New Age movement for a variety of reasons, including:

- Its spirit of unconditional acceptance. They are attracted to the god of the New Age, who ostensibly does not judge, and to New Agers, who are open-minded about the spiritual path they have chosen.
- The consciousness-altering experiences offered by techniques such as sensory-deprivation tanks, yoga, past-life regression, out-of-body experiences, and so forth.
- The emphasis on gaining wellness through natural means.
- The theme of personal development and self-improvement.
- The theme of power and control. Astrology, Tarot card readings, and other forms of parapsychology claim

to offer a glimpse into the future. The lure is that if I can see into the future, I can control my destiny.

■ Getting in touch with the mystical, the mysterious, and the spiritual secrets of ancient cultures.

■ The filling of a social void. We live in an alienated society, and the New Age movement provides an identity and reason for likeminded people to gather.

■ The filling of a spiritual void. Many in the New Age movement have climbed the ladder of success and found it led nowhere. Shirley MacLaine wrote, *"There has to be something more* is a refrain all too often echoed" among people in today's society.[11]

■ It gives meaning to life. It answers the questions, "Who am I?" "Why am I here?" and "Why is there suffering?" It also provides something outside of oneself to live for, in the form of a way to transform the world.

Question 6

In conjunction with Eric Buehrer, the Spiritual Counterfeits Project (SCP; a Christian organization that researches new religions) has produced an excellent article that outlines steps to take when encountering a situation like that described in question 6. Eric Buehrer is the executive vice president for Citizens for Excellence in Education, which is devoted to organizing and training Christians throughout the United States to become aware of the issues and to speak up concerning public education. (See the bibliography for their address.) Here is Buehrer/SCP's advice. You may want to let your group evaluate it and compare it to what the group came up with.

If you as a parent want to exempt your child from a class or cancel a program, the first step is to contact the teacher and explain your reasons for making your request. If the teacher refuses to comply, approach the school principal with a more formal request. If it is still denied, collect other parents and approach the principal again, with a unified voice. If your request is still denied, take your case to district administrators, school board members, and the local media.

Your request for cancellation of the program should

be based on two lines of argument: the religious nature of the material or practice and its "questionable educational value."[12] Both arguments require some research and preparation.

Concerning the religious argument, demonstrate that the New Age movement is a religion in that it answers the ultimate questions: "Who is God?" "Who is man?" and "What is the nature of and solution to humanity's problem?" The Constitution does not allow any religion to be promoted in the public schools.

The National Association of Evangelicals offers a booklet entitled "Religion in the Public School Curriculum: Questions and Answers," which delineates the difference between *teaching about* religion and *promoting* a religion in public schools. Some of those differences include:

■ The school may sponsor *study* about religion, but may not sponsor the *practice* of religion.
■ The school may *expose* students to a diversity of religious views, but may not *impose* any particular view.
■ The school may *educate* about all religion, but may not *promote* or *denigrate* any religion.
■ The school may *inform* the student about various beliefs, but should not seek to *conform* him or her to any particular belief.[13]

To use the argument about the program's lack of educational value, establish the point that "(1) the program does not impart the skills it claims to and/or (2) is based on speculative or fanciful theories."[14]

Most often, teachers encourage students to do the kind of exercise described in question 6 in order to enhance their ability to be creative or increase their ability to relax. One study found, however, that in tests of creativity, teachers of Transcendental Meditation "scored worse or only as well as control groups." The study stated, "It's possible, then, that all the effort to promote biofeedback gadgets, alpha machines and meditation, transcendental or otherwise, may have the side effect of decreasing our ability to think creatively."[15] Other research has found that "meditation may interfere with a person's logical, left-hemisphere processes," which would "reduce the chance of the meditator's producing a recognizably creative product."[16]

As far as the claims that meditation relaxes people, sitting quietly on a regular basis would do just as well. One physiological study of TM found that "the simple act of resting every day over a three-month period may produce more alpha waves than meditation."[17] Such simple periods of relaxation would not carry the Eastern religious overtones found in the case study, which go beyond teaching about a particular religion to promoting it.

Other reasons for challenging the appropriateness of such a program in a public school include (1) the program's lack of relevance to the subject being taught and (2) the program not being in the field in which the teacher is credentialed.[18]

For those who are concerned about the influence of the New Age in business, the Spiritual Counterfeits Project has produced a journal, "Minding the Store: Influences of the New Age in Business" (see bibliography), that addresses those issues. The journal includes a review of a valuable book entitled *Enhancing Human Performance: Issues, Theories, and Techniques.* The book documents the conclusions of a group of fifteen experts and scientists who had objectively researched the effectiveness of such techniques as biofeedback, accelerated learning, altered states of awareness, neuro-linguistic programming, hemispheric synchronization, stress reduction, relaxation response, guided imagery, ESP, remote viewing, and others. Many of the techniques studied have also made their way into the public schools, so this book has relevance for that area of concern as well. Richard Watring, who reviewed the book, writes that the "results [of the study] are not at all favorable to the New Age cause. The study points out the lack of empirical support for claims made, and it identifies many of the false assumptions which often inform programs and techniques."[19]

NOTES

1. W. W. Bartley, III, *Werner Erhard: The Transformation of a Man, The Founding of est* (New York: Clarkson N. Potter, Inc., 1978), pages 195-196.
2. *The Lifespring Family News: Founder's Edition,* vol. 1, no. 1 (San Rafael, CA: Lifespring, n.d.), page 3.
3. *Reasons or Results? Questions and Answers about the LIFESPRING Basic Training* (San Rafael, CA: Lifespring, n.d.), page 7.
4. *Lifespring Family News: Founder's Edition,* page 4.
5. Alice J. Porter, "Experiencing Lifespring," *Willamette Week,* October 24, 1977, page 2.
6. Quoted in Rick Fields, et al., eds., *Chop Wood, Carry Water* (Los Angeles, CA: J. P. Tarcher, 1984), page 82.
7. Frances Adeney, "Educators Look East," *SCP Journal,* vol. 5, no. 1 (Winter 1981-1982), page 29.
8. *The Aquarian Conspiracy: Personal and Social Transformation in the 1980s* (Los Angeles, CA: J. P. Tarcher, 1980), page 182.
9. Michael Talbot, *Mysticism and the New Physics* (New York: Bantam Books, 1981), page 14.
10. Gary Zukav, *The Dancing Wu Li Masters* (New York: William Morrow and Company, Inc., 1979), page 102.
11. Shirley MacLaine, *Going Within: A Guide for Inner Transformation* (New York: Bantam Books, 1989), page 26.
12. Eric Buehrer and Robert Burrows, "Challenging the New Age in Education," *SCP Newsletter,* vol. 14, no. 2 (1989), page 3.
13. "Religion in the Public School Curriculum: Questions and Answers" (available through the National Association of Evangelicals, 1023 - 15th St., N.W., Suite 500, Washington, DC 20005).
14. Buehrer, page 4.
15. Colin Martindale, "What Makes Creative People Different," *Psychology Today* (July 1975), page 50; see also David Haddon and Vail Hamilton, *TM Wants You!* (Grand Rapids, MI: Baker Book House, 1976), chapter 3.
16. Gary Schwartz, "The Facts on Transcendental Meditation: Part II," *Psychology Today* (April 1974), page 43.
17. Leon S. Otis, "The Facts on Transcendental Meditation: Part III," *Psychology Today* (April 1974), page 46.
18. Buehrer, page 4.
19. Richard Watring, "Producing Results: Fact and Fantasy," *SCP Journal,* vol. 9, no. 1 (1989), page 29.

THE CHRISTIAN RESPONSE

Goals

1. To provide a time for the participants to openly share their fears about and successes in evangelism.
2. To encourage Christians to reach out and talk to New Agers, breaking down the stereotypes New Agers have of us.
3. To help the group realize that they have some good news to share with New Agers, and to get them excited about sharing that good news.

Question 1

This is a warm-up, a chance for you to take the group members' emotional temperature, then go deeper with question 2. Again, humorous answers are great for releasing tension. You should expect that evangelism will not be everyone's favorite pastime; many believers feel guilty about this.

Question 2

Expect excuses and justifications, many of which are quite realistic. Try to draw forth the obstacles to reaching out that people face, perhaps with a follow-up question, such as: "What hinders you from being enthusiastic about reaching out? What obstacles are in your way?"

Common answers include fear and the lack of time.
Time is a serious issue, but it isn't a factor when you work
or otherwise spend time with people. A believer who spends
no time at all around the lost may want to examine his or her
priorities.

However, the purpose of this session is not to con-
vince your group that they should reach out, but that they
can—they have the necessary resources. You might want to
plan another session to deal with strategy issues such as time.

Question 4

Most people are led to the Lord through a friend or parent,
someone who took the time to get to know them and gain
their respect and confidence. Even if some went forward
during a crusade, camp meeting, or church service, it's still
most likely that a friend or parent brought them to the point
of making that decision.

What made these people qualified to share the gospel?
First, they had a vital relationship with the Lord themselves.
Second, they knew the person as a friend. Third, they understood the message of salvation. That's all the training it takes
to be an evangelist.

Question 5

Ephesians 6:19-20. Paul, the tireless evangelist to the Gentiles, asked those in the church at Ephesus to pray that he
would be fearless when proclaiming the gospel. Apparently
fear was a real possibility for Paul, and he needed divine help
to overcome it.

Second Timothy 1:6-8. To those in the group who tend to be
shy, it should be comforting to know that Timothy had to
deal with being timid (compare with 1 Corinthians 16:10-11,
1 Timothy 4:12). Nevertheless, Paul had confidence that
Timothy could do the job (1 Timothy 4:12). In these verses,
Paul also reveals that even if a person has a gift from God,
that gift still needs to be "fanned," or developed. Many Christians give up all too soon when attempting to develop their
evangelistic skills.

Matthew 28:19-20. According to this passage, evangelism is not an option for the Church, but a command. Jesus did not give us that command and leave us powerless to fulfill it, though, for He said, "Surely I am with you always, to the very end of the age." Evangelism must always be the primary objective of the Church, and each Christian must find his or her own way of fulfilling that objective.

Question 6
Some of the stereotypes that New Agers have of Christians are that we are anti-intellectual, judgmental, and hypocritical. New Agers also believe that Christians are not interested in listening to them.

Questions 7 and 8
Paul's primary concern in 1 Corinthians 9:19-23 is being unnecessarily offensive to the people he was trying to win to Christ. He uses as an example his attempts to reach those who are "under the law." When in such a situation, Paul does not flagrantly break the law to show them that Jesus had fulfilled the law and they are no longer in bondage to the law. Instead, he, like Jesus, befriends sinners "so that by all possible means [he] might save some."

How is Paul's principle of not being unnecessarily offensive relevant to the way we should approach New Agers? Could we join them in their concern for environmental issues, for human rights, or for social justice? Can we avoid making major issues out of such things as the validity of reincarnation, chakras, yoga, pyramid power, crystals, and so forth?

While I am very aware that such teachings and practices are fundamentally opposed to Christian theology, they can often lead to our fighting minor skirmishes and unnecessarily alienating the New Ager while neglecting the major battle, which is to get our New Age friend to realize that he or she stands condemned before a Holy God and needs a Savior. In other words, if we approach a New Ager with the intent of proving that reincarnation or yoga or crystals are not valid, we might win the argument, but we will have missed the more fundamental concepts that those things represent and that the person will more than likely continue to hold. (In Acts 9:19-25, Paul learned that he could win all the arguments and still fail to win anybody to Christ.)

In the introduction to the next session, I mention a young lady who confronted me by saying, "I don't believe God is a person, and I don't believe He will judge us, and I don't believe that we only have one chance." She threw several issues at me that could have quickly turned our discussion into an argument. Instead of picking up on those issues, though, I picked up on the fundamental issue that stood behind her statements—the Personhood of God. God's Personhood is the major issue when it comes to helping New Agers see the sense behind the biblical way of salvation.

Question 10

The New Age has its replacement for virtually every aspect of the Christian gospel. Instead of transformation through the regeneration of the Holy Spirit, the New Age offers transformation through the changing of our belief system or world view. In place of a personal relationship with God, the New Age offers a personal spirit-guide. Instead of the revelation of the Bible, the New Age offers revelation through UFOs, ascended masters, channeled messages, psychic powers, and personal intuition. In place of the Kingdom of God that will be introduced by the return of Jesus Christ, the New Age offers a golden age that will be ushered in by humanity. Instead of a Christian gospel of sinners saved by grace, the New Age offers a gospel of the ignorant being saved by knowledge.

The god of this age offers a gospel that looks attractive and promising but is spiritually bankrupt. Take out-of-body experiences (OBEs) as an example. OBEs offer the power to travel throughout not only the universe but also throughout other dimensions and realities. Robert Monroe, one of the foremost researchers of OBEs, has developed a technique called Hemi-Sync, which synchronizes the two hemispheres of the brain by using sound.[1] Some of those who have experienced Hemi-Sync claim it has produced "relief from insomnia, pain, and drug abuse; rapid physical healing; accelerated learning; enhanced creativity; stress reduction; even improved tennis and golf."[2]

Monroe has developed several steps for entering an OBE. First, you empty your mind. Second, you chant and breath rhythmically. Third, you say "the Gateway Affirmation," which says that you are more than your body and that you desire assistance from beings "whose wisdom is equal to or greater than my own."[3] Monroe said some of the people who went through his program reported that these beings, when asked about God, "were politely evasive, as if to say, 'You'll grow out of that concept eventually.'"[4] Such is the spiritual deception that can be encountered during these experiences and that can lead to spiritual bankruptcy.

NOTES

1. Jean-Noel Bassior, "Astral Travel," *New Age Journal* (November-December, 1988), pages 44-49, 84-85, 96-100.
2. Bassior, page 47.
3. Bassior, page 49.
4. Bassior, page 99.

THE GOD
OF THE NEW AGE

Goals

1. To become aware that the Personhood of God is a basic issue when it comes to reaching New Agers and discerning the biblical perspective on New Age concepts.
2. To think about the implications of whether God is an impersonal force or a personal Being.
3. To draw out those implications about God in the specific contexts of the meaning of love and the meaning of judgment.

Question 1a

Since the primary problem is that of a false belief in separation, the solution—and immediate goal—lies in the individual becoming aware of his or her essential unity with the oneness of God. The ultimate goal is to disassociate oneself from all things separate and to become identified with the oneness. The New Age movement sees this as a process of expansion, where the individual consciousness ultimately merges into the universal mind.

Question 1b

No. Moral issues are not relevant when it comes to relating to an impersonal force, because an impersonal force does not make moral distinctions. You can't slander electricity. In the New Age belief system, no matter how immoral we might be, we are still extended from the substance of god.

New Agers do, however, talk about the possibility of a person causing the flow of the divine current to be blocked. Ignorance and negative attitudes cause such blockages. Still, saying that ignorance or negative attitudes block the flow of psychic current is very different from saying that moral rebellion breaks the relationship between the sinner and the Holy God.

How are they different? It's in the way guilt is dealt with. New Agers would say that if I am bitter toward a person who received a promotion I felt I deserved, that bitterness might block the flow of the psychic current. I could not, however, restore the flow by confessing my bitterness to the universal energy. That energy, like any impersonal force, is oblivious both to my situation and to such moral distinctions. Instead, I need to work on my attitude.

If God is personal and holy, though, then guilt over jealousy and envy breaks my fellowship with Him. The way to deal with that guilt is by confessing my attitude of bitterness to God. Only then can our fellowship be restored.

Question 2

Brooks Alexander, formerly a senior researcher with the Spiritual Counterfeits Project, wrote:

> If God is a person, that means he wants Reality to be a certain way rather than another. Among other things, that translates into moral absolutes for us. The really bad news is that humanity's alienation from God has occurred at precisely that level of character and relationship. More specifically, it has occurred at the point of God's character that is moral and ethical—theology calls it the "holiness" of God. Human beings remain fatally alienated from their Creator until they have faced the moral dimensions of God's character and evaluated themselves in its light.[1]

Question 3
God is impersonal: Our problem is falsely believing that we are separate from God.

God is personal: Our problem is moral rebellion against a Holy God.

Question 4
Some of the images that might be mentioned are a mother nursing her baby, two sweethearts walking on a beach, a husband and wife celebrating their fiftieth wedding anniversary, a father playing ball with his son.

Question 5
Your images in question 4 were probably all interpersonal. Some people might come up with the image of a master's love for his dog or a patriot's love for his country. Wouldn't they also be considered images of love? Yes, but probably not the epitome of love. They would be better classified as devotion or loyalty.

Question 6
This section on love (questions 4-6) is designed to provide an approach that a Christian could use to lead a New Ager to the realization that if God is loving, then He must be personal, because love is inherently interpersonal. Love just doesn't fit in the context of an impersonal force. Stephen Hawkings, the famous astrophysicist, was correct when he responded to Shirley MacLaine's question, "Well, isn't harmonic energy loving?" Hawkings said, "I don't know that there is anything loving about energy. I don't think *loving* is a word I could ascribe to the universe."[2]

The key difference is that while the New Age god is not even aware of our suffering, the biblical God has entered into it, carried it upon Himself, still grieves with us for it, and has done and is doing something to end it. Which of these sounds like real love?

Questions 7 and 8
The two different views of God that Dr. Siegel has expressed—Heaven (which implies a personal God) or the original source

of energy—make a world of difference when it comes to what the afterlife will be like. If God is only the original source of energy, then the ultimate end of the individual is to expand into the universal oneness, which really means that the individual disappears as a separate person. Rajneesh said, "You will never encounter God. If you are there, God is not there because the seed [ego] is there. When you disappear, God is there; so there is no encounter really. . . . When YOU are not, God is there—emptiness in your hand, then God is there."[3] Aldous Huxley once said, "To know the ultimate Not-Self, which transcends the other not-selves and the ego . . . this is the consummation of human life, the end and ultimate purpose of individual existence."[4]

What would such an existence be like? According to *A Course in Miracles,* which is a channeled work, the person would be absorbed into a "Divine Abstraction,"[5] where there are no distinctions,[6] where no words are communicated,[7] and where there are no events—only a static, eternal now.[8]

Such a state sounds more like eternal death than eternal life. The New Age god, then, has committed the ultimate form of judgment. All existence is ultimately an illusion that will eventually be merged into the oneness that is god: no exceptions allowed.

On the other hand, if God is personal, then the afterlife will consist of eternal fellowship with Him for those who have trusted Jesus as their Savior. Jesus said, "This is eternal life: that they may know you, the only true God, and Jesus Christ, whom you have sent" (John 17:3). He also said, "In my Father's house are many rooms; if it were not so, I would have told you. I am going there to prepare a place for you. And if I go and prepare a place for you, I will come back and take you to be with me that you also may be where I am" (John 14:2-3). Paul speaks of his desire to "depart" and "be with Christ" (Philippians 1:23). The Apostle John described his vision of the age to come with these words, "Then I saw a new heaven and a new earth, for the first heaven and the first earth had passed away. . . . And I heard a loud voice from the throne saying, 'Now the dwelling of God is with men, and he will live with them. They will be his people, and God himself will be with them and be their God'" (Revelation 21:1,3).

Yes, the Bible speaks of those who will be condemned to eternal separation from God, but it also says that the God of the Bible "is patient with you, not wanting anyone to perish, but everyone to come to repentance" (2 Peter 3:9). God, moreover, loved us enough to provide the way of salvation by sending His one and only Son, Jesus Christ. God longs to have a relationship with us. He will not, however, coerce us into that relationship.

Question 9

What does the New Ager say he is assured of at death? In an immediate sense, reincarnation. He will either be born back into this physical realm as another person or graduate to another spiritual level. Either way, he will continue to pay for his karma, even though he doesn't remember what it was he did in his past lives.

In the more ultimate sense, the New Ager is assured of merging into an impersonal oneness. The New Ager might consider such an outcome to be the expansion of his consciousness into God-consciousness, but when God is an impersonal oneness without distinctions, ultimately the New Ager's individual consciousness is expanded into oblivion.

What is the Christian assured of at death? He's assured of being immediately ushered into God's presence, to be in eternal fellowship with Him. Eventually, all believers will receive resurrected bodies.

NOTES

1. Brooks Alexander, "Mysticism, Science & Biblical Faith," *SCP Newsletter*, vol. 13, no. 2 (1988), page 13.
2. Shirley MacLaine, *Going Within* (New York: Bantam Books, 1989), page 252.
3. Bhagwan Shree Rajneesh, *The Mustard Seed* (San Francisco, CA: Harper & Row, 1975), page 23.
4. Rick Fields, et al., eds., *Chop Wood, Carry Water* (Los Angeles, CA: J. P. Tarcher, 1984), page 19.
5. *A Course in Miracles: Text* (Tiburon, CA: Foundation for Inner Peace, 1975), page 64.
6. *A Course in Miracles: Text*, pages 64, 135; *A Course in Miracles: Workbook for Students*, page 311.
7. *A Course in Miracles: Manual for Teachers*, page 51.
8. *Text*, page 73; *Workbook*, page 443; Dean Halverson, "A Course in Miracles: Seeing YourSelf as Sinless," *SCP Journal*, vol. 7, no. 1 (1987), page 27.

CHANNELERS
AND SPIRIT-GUIDES

Goals
1. To define channeling and understand the void that it fills in the New Ager.
2. To understand why the Bible prohibits spiritism.
3. To articulate the role of the Holy Spirit and to appreciate the differences between the Holy Spirit and channeled spirits.

Pages 25-26

William Kautz and Melanie Branon represent the intuition theory of channeling and define it as "an inner process, an intuitive connection with a universal but unseen source of information and insight. . . . Knowledge that lies beyond conscious awareness can . . . flow freely into the mind and be conveyed through speaking or writing to others."[1]

Jon Klimo tends more toward the personalized entity theory: "Channeling is the communication of information to or through a physically embodied human being from a source that is said to exist on some other level or dimension of reality than the physical as we know it, and that is not from the normal mind (or self) of the channel."[2]

Sarah Thomason, who is a linguist, listened to eleven

channelers and observed that "all had inconsistent pronun-
ciation or implausible accents and dialects for the time and
place they supposedly lived."[3] For example, Marjorie Turcott
channels an entity named Matthew, who supposedly lived in
Scotland during the sixteenth century. Thomason noticed that
Turcott, when speaking in Matthew's voice, uses the term
rapscallion, which was not used in Scotland until two hundred years after Matthew's time. He uses another term, *bully
boy,* to mean "tyrannical coward," but during the sixteenth
century in Scotland, it meant "good friend." Plus, Matthew's
channeled voice keeps the *gh,* as in the word *neighbor,* silent,
whereas Scots have always pronounced it as a "ch."[4]

Thomason also listened to Penny Torres, who channels
Mafu a first-century leper, and observed that she speaks with
a British accent, but the British accent dates back no further
than AD 800. Thomason also finds it unusual that Ramtha,
a 35,000-year-old warrior from Atlantis channeled by J. Z.
Knight, speaks with an accent that is in usage today. She
says these two examples—Mafu and Ramtha—are "either
an unprecedented linguistic coincidence, or Knight and Torres are inventing language for their channeling routines."[5]
Thomason concluded her study by saying that the "speech
patterns shed considerable doubt on their legitimacy."[6]

Concerning New Agers who are encouraging others to
contact their spirit-guides, Gary Zukav has written,

> Remind yourself that you are supported, that you are not
> going it alone upon this Earth. Dwell in the company of
> your nonphysical Teachers and guides. . . . Do not fear
> dependency. What is wrong with being dependent upon
> the Universe, whether that is your Teachers or Divine
> Intelligence? . . . Delight in the dependency. Give your
> guides and Teachers permission to come closer.[7]

Question 1
Shirley MacLaine answers the question about the void
that channeling fills when she writes, "When I go within
I look for communication and guidance . . . and in general have a friendly exchange with someone or something

which I perceive to be more advanced than 'I' perceive myself."[8]

Because the New Age god is impersonal, it is unable to communicate with us. *A Course in Miracles* says, "God does not understand words, for they were made by separated minds to keep them in the illusion of separation."[9] It would be difficult, to say the least, to have a meaningful relationship with such a god. By seeking communication and guidance from spirit-guides or ascended masters, New Agers are replacing God with an intermediate source.

Question 2

If you show Genesis 3 to a New Ager, let these similarities speak for themselves and give him the freedom to make the connection about the source of New Age teachings for himself.

What are the similarities?

■ "You will not surely die" (Genesis 3:4). New Agers deny that anyone ever really dies, and they deny that God judges anyone.

■ "When you eat of it your eyes will be opened" (verse 5). The key to transformation in the New Age movement is in the eyes, or sight, which in more current terminology would be called perception, belief system, self-image, paradigm, or world view.

■ "You will be like God" (verse 5). According to the New Age movement, we are all divine and have the potential to be as powerful as God. Shirley MacLaine says, "Since there is no separateness, we are each God-like, and God is in each of us. . . . We are literally made up of God energy, therefore we can create whatever we want in life because we are each co-creating with the energy of God—the energy that makes the universe itself."[10]

■ "Knowing good and evil" (verse 5). Adam and Eve knew good and evil in the sense that they usurped God's moral authority and decided what would be good and evil themselves. Since the New Age relegates God to the level of an impersonal oneness without moral distinctions, humanity becomes the highest standard for judging right and wrong. There are, then, no moral absolutes.

NOTES

1. William Kautz and Melanie Branon, *Channeling: The Intuitive Connection* (San Francisco, CA: Harper & Row, 1987), pages 2-3.
2. Jon Klimo, *Channeling* (New York: J. P. Tarcher, 1987), page 2.
3. Marjory Roberts, "A Linguistic 'Nay' to Channeling," *Psychology Today* (October 1989), page 64.
4. Roberts, page 64.
5. Roberts, page 64.
6. Roberts, page 64.
7. Gary Zukav, *The Seat of the Soul* (New York: Simon & Schuster, 1989), pages 239-240.
8. Shirley MacLaine, *Going Within* (New York: Bantam Books, 1989), page 70.
9. *A Course in Miracles: Manual for Teachers* (Tiburon, CA: Foundation for Inner Peace, 1975), vol. 3, page 51.
10. MacLaine, page 85.

NEW AGE HEALING

Goals
1. To discover and discuss the variety of theories people hold concerning the mind's effect on the body.
2. To acknowledge that we might be able to agree with the New Age movement in some of the issues it addresses, but also to be aware of its hidden spiritual agenda.
3. To distinguish between the New Age meaning of faith and the Christian meaning.

Question 1
The purpose of this exercise is not to come up with a definitive statement about the mysterious relationship between the mind and the body, but to help people see the variety of opinions others have. Limit the discussion to five or ten minutes maximum.

Question 3
Both the New Age movement and Christianity affirm that spiritual problems can be the source of physical problems. They differ, however, in that the New Age movement has no understanding of a Holy God who can be grieved by our sin, or of confessing our sin before God as a way of dealing with our spiritual problems.

Question 5

The primary issue here is the object of faith. Whether it's explicit or not, faith always has an object. With New Agers, the object of faith is either the influence of the mind on the body or the idea that we are inherently perfect and by dwelling on that perfection, we can be physically healthy.

When Jesus talked about faith, however, it was clear that He was to be the object of faith. He said, "Trust in God; trust also in me" (John 14:1). When talking with Martha about the death of Lazarus, He made belief in Him the single most important issue: "Jesus said to her, 'I am the resurrection and the life. He who believes in me will live, even though he dies; and whoever lives and believes in me will never die. *Do you believe this?*'" (John 11:25-26, italics added). In a similar incident, after healing the man who had been blind since birth, Jesus again made belief in Him the primary issue,

> He said, "Do you believe in the Son of Man?"
>
> "Who is he, sir?" the man asked. "Tell me so that I may believe in him."
>
> Jesus said, "You have now seen him; in fact, he is the one speaking with you."
>
> Then the man said, "Lord, I believe," and he worshiped him. (John 9:35-38)

Lastly, Jesus said, "The work of God is this: to believe in the one he has sent" (John 6:29).

Question 6

The problem would be in the strength of one's faith, that is, one's attitude. If we have the potential to heal ourselves, then we are the ones to blame if that healing does not occur.

A three-and-one-half-year medical study reported in *The New England Journal of Medicine* challenges the popular New Age belief that positive mental attitudes significantly affect serious diseases such as cancer.[1] Over the study period, medical researchers followed the progress of 204 patients who had an advanced form of cancer and 155 patients whose melanoma or breast cancer had gone into remission. Each patient was asked about his or her mental attitude and scored on a scale that ranged from low to middle to high. During the course of the study period, 154 (75 percent) of those with advanced cancer died and 41 (26 percent) of those whose cancer had gone into remission had recurrences. What is most significant about this study is that the researchers found no correlation between a good mental attitude and the number of deaths or recurrences. Just as many of those with high mental attitudes died or had recurrences of cancer as those with low mental attitudes.

Dr. Marcia Angell, editor of the *New England Journal of Medicine,* made some insightful comments concerning the belief that positive attitudes can cure serious diseases. She said that this belief is unfortunate for a couple of reasons. First, it may draw the patient away from a more conventional form of therapy that might help him. Second, if a patient sincerely believes that his positive mental attitude will cure his disease, then when the disease persists, he will blame himself.

Angell quoted from one person's journal entry that was dated a year before she died of tuberculosis: "A bad day . . . horrible pains and so on, and weakness. I could do nothing. The weakness was not only physical. I must *heal my Self* before I will be well. This must be done alone and at once. It is at the root of my not getting better. My mind is not *controlled*."[2] Angell comments that the "view of sickness and death as a personal failure is a particularly unfortunate form of blaming the victim. At a time when patients are already burdened by disease, they should not be further burdened by having to accept responsibility for the outcome."[3]

Yet it is precisely that burden of responsibility that the New Age and the holistic health movements produce.

In an interview with the *New Age Journal,* transpersonal psychologist Ken Wilber criticized the New Age approach to healing: "I call it neotrogenic guilt—guilt caused by the new age mentality. You create your own reality, your thoughts are in control of the entire world, and, thus, if you get a disease of any sort, you have caused it."[4]

Wilber continues by saying that the primary mistake

of the New Age approach to disease is that it is a one-level approach rather than a multilevel one, the levels being the spiritual, mental, emotional, psychological, and physical.

> By thinking that all disease has its origins solely or exclusively on the spiritual level, you actually and completely cease looking for causes on the physical. And therefore you give up or bypass or fail to take advantage of physical-level cures, which are, in fact, the only ones that are going to work for genuinely physical-level diseases.[5]

Question 7

How would a Christian approach the situation of not being healed? The Christian camp is not monolithic when it comes to answering this and the following question. My intention in asking these questions is not to be divisive but to delineate the basic differences between the Christian approach to faith and the New Age approach.

New Agers have placed their faith in the *principle* of their inner perfection and in the *power* of the mind to create reality. *Principle* and *power* are words that carry guarantees. They are cause-and-effect words. If you have an adequate cause (positive attitudes), the effect (health) will automatically be produced.

In Christianity, however, the object of our faith is not an impersonal principle or power, but a *Person*—the Person of Jesus Christ. When you place your faith in the Person of Jesus Christ, you do so largely on the basis that you know He loves you because He died for you. That love does not guarantee that He will produce everything you ask of Him. This type of faith becomes a matter of trusting the Person of God, no matter what the immediate circumstances.

Question 8

There is a "now and not yet" quality to the Kingdom of God. Through faith in Jesus Christ, the future rule of God becomes a reality in our hearts during this present age of darkness, but the full extent of that rule (God's Kingdom) is yet to come. Only then will physical healing be guaranteed for all believers, when "the perishable [will be] clothed with the imperishable, and the mortal with immortality" (1 Corinthians 15:54).

The following chart outlines much of what has been discussed in questions 4-8.

NEW AGE	CHRISTIANITY
The Meaning of Faith	
Faith is a trust in the healing powers of the mind and the idea that in our true selves we have perfect health.	Faith is a trust in the love and wisdom of the Person of God.
The Results of Faith	
Results of faith are guaranteed, because faith is based on predictable forces.	Results of faith are not guaranteed in this lifetime, because faith is based on God's sovereign and loving will.
The Meaning of Failure	
Failure to be healed reveals a lack of faith or very possibly a spiritual defect.	Failure to be healed does not alter one's confidence in God because He has guaranteed healing in *His* time.

Question 9

When he or she has fully realized and manifested the perfection within or is able to maintain a positive attitude 100 percent of the time. Or when he has no more lessons to learn or has burned off his karma. In other words, there is no assurance.

Charles Fillmore's story is relevant here. In 1889, Charles and Myrtle Fillmore founded the metaphysical church known as the Unity School of Christianity. They based their movement on the belief that the mind has tremendous healing powers. Charles became so convinced of the healing powers of the mind that he predicted in the *Unity* magazine that he would not die. He was ninety-two years old. Subscribers questioned him concerning this fantastic assertion, and he responded by stating his prediction even more strongly,

Subscribers are now asking if I mean that I shall live forever in the flesh body. . . . I expect to associate with those in the flesh and be known as the same person that I have been for ninety-two years, but my body will be changed in appearance from that of an old man to a young man with a perfectly healthy body.[6]

Fillmore died a few months later.

Question 10

If a New Ager should need healing, pray that God will heal him or her. It is in precisely this kind of evangelistic situation that God loves to reveal Himself.

NOTES
1. B. R. Cassileth, et al., "Psychosocial Correlates of Survival in Advanced Malignant Disease," *The New England Journal of Medicine,* vol. 312, no. 24 (June 13, 1985), pages 1551-1555.
2. Marcia Angell, "Psychosocial Correlates of Survival in Advanced Malignant Disease," page 1571.
3. Angell, page 1572.
4. Ken and Treya Wilber, "Do We Make Ourselves Sick?: A Conversation with Ken Wilber," *New Age Journal* (September/October 1988), page 51.
5. Wilber, page 51.
6. J. D. Freeman, *The Story of Unity* (Unity Village, MO: Unity, 1972), pages 210-211.

WHAT'S THE BIG DEAL ABOUT SIN?

Goals

1. To see that if God is impersonal, then moral sin is not an issue; but if God is personal, then sin is an issue.
2. To understand that the dynamics of interpersonal relationships are useful as a way of illustrating the meaning of sin to a New Ager.
3. To understand the attitude at the root of sin and why sin alienates us from God.

Page 37

A technique called "centering" approaches guilt in a way that is similar to the way Gateways Institute approaches it: "Anytime that you have something in your head that you don't like, breathe it out and then replace it with pure, clean energy when you breathe in."[1]

Question 1

Gateways Institute is apparently saying that guilt can be dealt with by the mind and is not something that must be dealt with between you and God.

By whom am I forgiven? According to New Agers, I am the source of my own forgiveness, because I am not morally accountable to anyone beyond myself.

On what basis am I forgiven? First, on the basis of my own change in perspective, and second, on the basis that I am divine in my true self and do not need forgiveness.

Question 2

What is missing? First, a morally Holy God. Second, the realization that sin causes alienation from God. Third, a sense of being personally culpable before God. Fourth, a sense that we need to confess our sins to God before we can receive forgiveness.

Question 3

If God is personal, the good news is that forgiveness is possible. Forgiveness is a relevant concept only in the context of personal and moral beings, where guilt and sin are real issues.

Question 4

If the god is impersonal, then forgiveness is not possible. If the god is an impersonal force within all things, then moral laws are the same as laws of nature, and one does not break a law of nature (such as the law of gravity) without paying the price.

The following chart will help clarify the good news and bad news about sin.

GOD IS AN IMPERSONAL ONENESS	GOD IS A PERSONAL BEING
Good News: Sin is not an issue with god and can be dealt with on the level of the human mind.	*Bad News:* Sin is real, and it causes us to be alienated from God.
Bad News: Forgiveness is not possible because moral laws become like laws of nature.	*Good News:* Forgiveness is possible because the source of moral law is founded in the Person of God, and persons can forgive.

Question 5

This question can produce discussion to help the group realize that this statement accurately represents the attitude

behind even the smallest sin. When we sin, we place ourselves above God, whether we are aware of doing so or not.

The New Age belief system lends itself to such an
attitude, because it denies that God is transcendent from (or
other than) His creation and that He is holy—the absolute
standard by which humanity will be judged. Instead, New
Agers characterize God as the essence of existence, the
life force within all things and a oneness without moral
distinctions.

What happens to morality, then? First, it becomes relative.
In describing the assumptions of the two approaches forming
the foundation of Values Clarification—a process of discovering
one's morals present in the public schools—Merrill Harmin and
Sidney Simon say they "are not based upon the assumption that
absolute good exists and can be known. They view values as
relative, personal, and situational."[2]

Werner Erhard's biographer describes the "distinctive
morality" that lies at "the heart . . . of Werner's perspective." He says that, according to Erhard's morality, "Right
action is contextually determined behavior; wrong action is
determined by position, by concepts"; and "to be appropriate,
to act appropriately, is to do what is fitting or suitable to a
situation."[3]

One New Age publication reported approvingly that
Allan Ginsberg asked a Tibetan tantric master,[4] "if there were
any 'special' teachings or sexual rituals for homosexuals."
The Tibetan master replied, "It's not so important if you
make love with a man or woman. The important thing is the
communication—whoever it is with."[5]

Second, morals are derived from one's experience, not
from an external authority. Values Clarification's main task
"is not to identify and transmit the 'right' values, but to help
a student clarify his own values."[6]

Secular humanism is very similar to New Age thinking
with respect to the derivation of morality and its relativity.
The signers of the Humanist Manifesto II stated in the third
point, "We affirm that moral values derive their source from
human experience. Ethics is autonomous and situational,
needing no theological or ideological sanction."[7]

Third, morality will be judged by its usefulness, not by any inherent sense of right and wrong. For example, people are beginning to choose monogamy not because it is inherently right, but to help prevent them from getting AIDS.

Question 6

Self-centeredness manifests itself as greed, lust, envy, exploitation, anger, slander, hatred, murder, and the desire for power and control (see Mark 7:21-22; 1 Corinthians 3:3, 6:9-10; Galatians 5:19-21).

In reporting on the Global Forum of Spiritual and Parliamentary Leaders on Human Survival (April 1988), Anuradha Vittachi says those in the Green political movement

> perceive the attitude of domination that manifests in our assault of nature also manifesting in our attitude toward people; if we come across people less powerful than ourselves, we tend to exploit or ignore them, rather than treat them as members of our human family. Thus, men use women, the rich enslave the poor, and industrial nations exploit the developing world.[8]

The Christian locates the source of this "attitude of domination" in our prideful and rebellious attitude toward God.

NOTES
1. Gay Hendricks and Russel Wills, *The Centering Book: Awareness Activities for Children & Adults to Relax the Body & Mind* (New York: Prentice-Hall Press, 1975), pages 12-13.
2. Merrill Harmin and Sidney Simon, "Values," in Sidney Simon and Howard Kirschenbaum, eds., *Readings in Values Clarification* (Minneapolis, MN: Winston Press, 1973), page 11.
3. W. W. Bartley, III, *Werner Erhard: The Transformation of a Man, The Founding of est* (New York: Clarkson N. Potter, Inc., 1978), pages 211-212.
4. Tantra is a form of yoga based on the powers of sexual energy.
5. Rick Fields, et al., eds., *Chop Wood, Carry Water* (Los Angeles, CA: J. P. Tarcher, 1984), page 70.
6. Harmin and Simon, page 11.
7. Corliss Lamont, *The Philosophy of Humanism* (New York: Continuum, 1988), page 293.
8. Anuradha Vittachi, *Earth Conference One* (Boston: Shambhala, 1989), page 36.

GOD LOVES YOU, BUT . . .

Goals

1. To clear up some fuzzy thinking about God's love.
2. To show that behind the unconditional love of the New Age god is the denial of the element of holiness.
3. To help Christians appreciate the kind of tough love that God has for us.

Questions 3-5

As we contrast the New Age and biblical meanings of "God is light" and "God is love," we see that the New Age has omitted holiness. This is not surprising because holiness discriminates, or judges, between right and wrong. Therefore, it causes God to be exclusive toward people, rather than inclusive.

Without holiness, the New Age god's love might be unconditional, but it is also naive and unrealistic. Even some in the New Age movement recognize the need to reintroduce discernment:

> It seems very popular in the American culture right now to think that love is accepting and trying to understand that everything (and anything) a person does and says is "perfect" and that there are no ultimate standards and

values, in other words, no right or wrong. We'd like to suggest that this concept has been taken to the extreme *ad nauseam*. There are jerks in this world, and it's okay to recognize them.[1]

If we have the right to acknowledge "the jerks," then how much more does God have that right!

What is the purpose of God's love in 1 John 4:8-10? As you study these verses, you will see that God's love is historical, incarnational, directional (*from* God *to* us), and sacrificial (in the sense of being substitutionary). Each one of those characteristics is aimed in some way at dealing with humanity's sin.

Questions 6 and 7

The New Age way of dealing with this dilemma is to emphasize God's love to the exclusion of His holiness. Even though Marcie attributed personal characteristics—such as love, intelligence, and consciousness—to the normally impersonal light, she did not attribute holiness. While such a god seems all-loving, he lets humanity try to deal with evil. We are the ones who suffer in this imperfect world, and all god has done is to encourage us to "learn the lesson of love."

History indicates, though, that humanity today is no closer to learning that lesson than it was 2000 years ago. How does the New Age god respond to our suffering? A Unity author[2] was uncharacteristically candid when he wrote,

God as the underlying substance of all things, God as principle, is unchanging, and does remain forever uncognizant [sic] of and unmoved by the changing things of time and sense. It is true that God as principle does not feel pain, is not moved by the cries of the children of men for help.[3]

The God of the Bible is quite different. In Exodus, for example, God says, "I have indeed seen the misery of my people in Egypt. I have heard them crying out because of their slave drivers, and I am concerned about their suffering.

So I have come down to rescue them from the hand of the Egyptians" (Exodus 3:7-8). Because the God of the Bible is holy, He is keenly aware of and concerned about the suffering caused by evil. He was concerned enough to break into history through Jesus,

> Who, being in very nature God,
> . . . made himself nothing,
>> taking the very nature of a servant,
>> being made in human likeness.
> And being found in appearance as a man,
>> he humbled himself
>> and became obedient to death—
>> even death on a cross! (Philippians 2:6-8)

Such a God is indeed able to sympathize with our suffering (see Hebrews 4:15).

Since God is holy, how can we who fall far short of that holiness be reconciled to Him? God has provided a way that not only reconciles us to Him, but also upholds both His holiness and His love. He takes our sins and places them on the sinless One, Jesus, who has already paid the penalty—death. It was just as Isaiah had prophesied:

> He was pierced for our transgressions,
>> he was crushed for our iniquities;
> the punishment that brought us peace was upon him,
>> and by his wounds we are healed.
> We all, like sheep, have gone astray,
>> each of us has turned to his own way;
> and the LORD has laid on him
>> the iniquity of us all. (Isaiah 53:5-6)

Through the death of Jesus Christ, God is both the "just and the one who justifies those who have faith in Jesus" (Romans 3:26).

Question 8
The Dalai Lama's words are appealing to that part of us that believes humanity's ability to love is sufficient to deal with

the troubles that plague us. But, while brotherly love is certainly needed, the power behind it must be rooted in God's transforming love. As John says, "This is love: not that we loved God, but that he loved us and sent his Son as an atoning sacrifice for our sins. Dear friends, since God so loved us, we also ought to love one another" (1 John 4:10-11).

NOTES
1. Robbyn and His Merrye Bande, "Unconditional Love: Confusion Over Judgment and Unconditional Love," *Body, Mind and Spirit,* no. 36, November/December 1989, page 50.
2. The metaphysical movement, which is the religious wing of the New Age movement, is based on the concept that mind is ultimate and that our minds have the power to change and even to create physical reality. The Unity School of Christianity, founded by Charles and Myrtle Fillmore, is part of that movement.
3. *Foundations of Unity,* Series Two, vol. 3 (Unity Village, MO: Unity, 1982), page 143.

OPEN-MINDEDNESS AND THE WAY TO GOD

Goals

1. To see that both the New Age movement and Christianity make claims to truth but that, without a doubt, both cannot be true.
2. To understand why the Bible says, "Small is the gate and narrow the road that leads to life, and only a few find it" (Matthew 7:14).
3. To discern the implications of the New Age belief that all paths lead to God.

Question 2

a. With respect to God:

NEW AGE	CHRISTIANITY
God is . . .	*God is . . .*
impersonal.	personal.
without moral distinctions.	morally holy.
one with the life force beneath creation.	distinct from creation.

b. With respect to humanity:

NEW AGE	CHRISTIANITY
Humanity is . . .	*Humanity is . . .*
divine, in that we are extended from God's essence.	made in God's image, but not extended from God's essence.
ignorant of our oneness, but not separated from God.	sinful and alienated from God.

c. With respect to life after death:

NEW AGE	CHRISTIANITY
Life after death is . . .	*Life after death is . . .*
spiritual progression to attain enlightenment.	spent in either heaven or hell.
expanding one's consciousness into the oneness.	either eternal fellowship with God or eternal separation from God.

Question 4

Financially, he was destitute. Physically, he was starving. Socially, he was ostracized. Most importantly, though, he was spiritually contrite: "Father, I have sinned against heaven and against you. I am no longer worthy to be called your son" (Luke 15:21).

Question 5

The parable and the statement illustrate the fact that salvation is not, as the New Agers would say, a matter of striving to attain or manifest our inner perfection. Instead, it is a matter of restoring one's relationship with a God whose presence and authority we have spurned. C. S. Lewis accurately described humanity's situation when he wrote, "Fallen man is not simply an imperfect creature who needs improvement: he is a rebel who must lay down his arms."[1] When it comes to ways to restore a relationship that we are responsible for breaking, there is really only one way to do it: through confessing our guilt and acknowledging our unworthiness to receive forgiveness.

NOTE
1. C. S. Lewis, *Mere Christianity* (New York: Macmillan, 1952), page 59.

THE UNIQUENESS OF JESUS

Goals
1. To understand why Jesus' uniqueness is important to Christianity and in what ways the Bible says He is unique.
2. To see how Jesus' resurrection is relevant for us today.
3. To understand that Christianity's central message is a relationship, not a religion, and that our Christ-filled lives are the most effective means by which our New Age friends will see the risen Lord.

Question 1
While New Agers don't deny that Jesus was exemplary in the extent to which He manifested His Christhood, they do deny that Jesus was uniquely related to God. If Jesus is not unique, we can admire Him, but we don't have to worship Him. The Bible says that Jesus was the unique Son of God (John 3:16), but New Agers say we are all sons of God. When Jesus' uniqueness is denied, then His life becomes significant primarily as an example, not as the substitute for our sin and the mediator between us and God. As an illustration of this New Age tendency to laud Jesus only as our example, one New Age publication entitled *The Universalian* has a logo that says: "God is the Center, Love is the Motive, Christ is the Example."[1]

Question 2

Jesus' uniqueness is important to Christians because it means that He was uniquely related to God as God's one and only Son. Moreover, since Jesus was uniquely related to God, His incarnation means that God loved us enough to reach down to us through His Son so that we could have a relationship with Him (see 1 John 4:9-10). Jesus' uniqueness also means that He is more than our example; He is our Savior.

Question 3

Assign each set of Scriptures to one or two group members. Give them a minute or two to look up the passages, then ask them to report back to the group on what they learned.

Question 4

It is ironic that New Agers either dismiss as historically untrue or spiritualize Jesus' physical resurrection from the dead (that is, say that Jesus rose spiritually, not physically). Yet they make a big deal about people who have dealt with death in ways that pale to insignificance when compared to the resurrection. Shirley MacLaine, for example, tells of a friend who was dying as a result of AIDS. He was angry at the doctors for not being able to heal the disease and angry with himself "for creating it." MacLaine spoke to him of the power of the body's energy centers (chakras), and he started to work with them. MacLaine reports that her friend stayed alive six months longer than the doctors had expected.[2]

As another example, one of the books that was popular during the early years of the New Age movement was Paramahansa Yogananda's *Autobiography of a Yogi,* which spoke of the powers of self-realization. On March 7, 1952, Yogananda died. At the beginning of his book appear excerpts from a letter by Mr. Harry Rowe, who was the mortuary director of Forest Lawn in Los Angeles at the time Yogananda died. Rowe reported, "No physical disintegration was visible in his body even twenty days after death," after which time he was buried.[3]

In contrast, Jesus didn't just live six months longer than

expected or escape decay for twenty days; He died and physically rose from the dead three days later.

Question 6

It confirms and supports the credibility of Jesus' claims. If Jesus had remained dead and buried, then His disciples would have dismissed Him as a failure, which is what they were about to do (Luke 24:11,21; John 20:25), and history would have disregarded His life altogether. Because He rose from the dead as He had predicted, though, His actions gave credence to His words. The choices are that He was either a lunatic, a liar, or the Lord. The character of His words and the nature of His works do not fit with the first two choices, but they are consistent with the last one.[4]

Question 7

Some of the key theological terms that occur in these verses are defined below:

■ *Justification* (Romans 3:21-26) means that Jesus paid the penalty for our legal debt before God and His righteous law.
■ *Imputation* (Romans 4:23-25) means Christ's righteousness was credited to our account.
■ *Redemption* (Romans 3:24, Ephesians 1:7) means we were bought with a price and freed from our slavery to sin.
■ *Reconciliation* (Colossians 1:19-22) means that the relationship between us and God is now restored, where before there was enmity.
■ *Atoning sacrifice,* or *propitiation* (1 John 4:10), means God's wrath against our sin was diverted in its entirety to Jesus Christ.[5]

Questions 8 and 9

Questions 8 and 9 include a lot of Scriptures covering the key elements of faith in Christ. You may not need to spend a lot of time on these if your group is saturated in biblical teaching. But if not, this may be a great opportunity to get a grip on the amazing "So what?" of faith in Christ.

Can we trust the Bible? Did the biblical authors accurately record the details of Jesus' life and teaching? Did the early Church embellish or distort the image of the historical Jesus for its own purposes? Since we do not have the original manuscripts, how can we be assured that the copies accurately reflect the originals?

Extrabiblical evidence, in the form of archaeological evidence and secular texts, supports the events of the New Testament.[6] The New Testament was written by Jesus' disciples or those close to them and distributed to eyewitnesses who could have refuted any distortions. The biblical authors also expressed an awareness of the importance of historical accuracy (Luke 1:1-4, John 21:24, 1 Corinthians 15:1-8, Hebrews 2:3-4, 2 Peter 1:16).

The books of the New Testament were written between twenty and sixty years after Jesus' resurrection, Galatians being the earliest (AD 49) and Revelation the latest (early 90s). The fact that Acts and the synoptic gospels (Matthew, Mark, and Luke) do not mention the destruction of Jerusalem in AD 70 indicates that they were probably written no later than that year. They very well might have been written as early as the mid-40s to mid-50s, which dates them to between fifteen and thirty years after Jesus' crucifixion (AD 30).[7] The gospels, moreover, were based on oral tradition and written manuscripts that existed even earlier.[8] In addition, the New Testament itself contains pre-New Testament creeds and hymns that further bridge the gap between the time of Jesus' life and the writing of the New Testament, in that they bring us down to the time of the very events themselves.

Finally, the copies of the original New Testament manuscripts are early, accurate, and numerous. New Testament scholar F. F. Bruce wrote,

> The evidence for our New Testament writings is ever so much greater than the evidence for many writings of classical authors, the authenticity of which no-one dreams of questioning. And if the New Testament were a collection of secular writings, their authenticity would

generally be regarded as beyond all doubt. It is a curious fact that historians have often been much readier to trust the New Testament records than have many theologians.[9]

The books listed below are helpful sources on the credibility of the biblical manuscripts and the historical accuracy of the Bible (see the bibliography for further sources):

■ F. F. Bruce, *The New Testament Documents: Are They Reliable?*
■ Craig Blomberg, *The Historical Reliability of the Gospels.*
■ R. T. France, *The Evidence for Jesus.*
■ Gary Habermas, *The Verdict of History: Conclusive Evidence for the Life of Jesus.*

While we are on the subject of the credibility of the biblical manuscripts, we should also mention the common belief among New Agers that a certain church council removed passages from the Bible that taught reincarnation. Kevin Ryerson, the channel that Shirley MacLaine consulted in *Out on a Limb,* said, "It's quite well known that the Council of Nicea voted to strike the teaching of reincarnation from the Bible."[10]

Ryerson's statement is mistaken at several points. First, the council at issue is not the one at Nicea, which took place in AD 325, but the Second Council of Constantinople, which took place in AD 553—over two hundred years later. Second, the only issue remotely related to that of reincarnation in that second council had to do with Origen's beliefs in the pre-existence of the soul. Some reincarnationists teach that the pre-existence doctrine implies reincarnation,[11] but Origen himself explicitly denied such an implication.[12] Third, there was never any talk of deleting passages from the biblical manuscripts, only of condemning as heretical Origen's pre-existence doctrine. Fourth, the biblical manuscripts that precede the Second Council of Constantinople do not differ in any significant way from those that follow it, which proves that no biblical passages were removed.[13]

NOTES

1. *The Universalian,* vol. 5, no. 4 (November/December 1989), page 1.
2. Shirley MacLaine, *Going Within* (New York: Bantam Books, 1989), pages 129-130.
3. Paramahansa Yogananda, *Autobiography of a Yogi* (Los Angeles, CA: Self-Realization Fellowship, 1968), page iv.
4. See C. S. Lewis, *Mere Christianity* (New York: Macmillan, 1952), page 59; Josh McDowell, *Evidence That Demands a Verdict* (Arrowhead Springs, CA: Campus Crusade for Christ, 1972), chapter 7.
5. For an excellent discussion of these terms, see Leon Morris, *The Atonement* (Downers Grove, IL: InterVarsity, 1983).
6. Edwin Yamauchi, "Archaeology and the New Testament," in Frank Gaebelein, ed., *The Expositor's Bible Commentary,* vol. 1 (Grand Rapids, MI: Zondervan, 1979), pages 647-669.
7. Gary Habermas, *The Verdict of History: Conclusive Evidence for the Life of Jesus* (Nashville, TN: Thomas Nelson, 1988), pages 151-154.
8. F. F. Bruce, *The New Testament Documents: Are They Reliable?* (Downers Grove, IL: InterVarsity, 1960), page 45.
9. Bruce, page 15.
10. Shirley MacLaine, *Out on a Limb* (New York: Bantam Books, 1983), page 181.
11. Joseph Head and S. L. Cranston, *Reincarnation: An East-West Anthology* (Wheaton, IL: Quest, 1961), page 39.
12. Mark Albrecht, *Reincarnation: A Christian Appraisal* (Downers Grove, IL: InterVarsity, 1982), pages 46-47.
13. Joseph Gudel, Robert Bowman, and Dan Schlesinger, "Reincarnation: Did the Church Suppress It?" *Christian Research Journal* (Summer 1987), page 12.

REACHING OUT TO NEW AGERS

When you approach the New Ager, your highest priority should be building a relationship. Understanding, not confrontation, is the order of the day. Because the New Age teaches that truth is relative according to the individual, your New Age friend must be approached *as an individual* in order to discover what he believes. Ask questions, and listen. Listening will in itself speak volumes about your love and concern for that person as an individual.

Ask your friend about his spiritual trek. Who influenced him to take such a spiritual path? What books or experiences were influential? In what spiritual practices is he involved? What's the theory or belief system behind those practices? What is the goal of his spiritual practices?

As he answers your questions, listen for the following:

■ words that indicate a belief in an impersonal force or divine energy;
■ inconsistencies in his thoughts about God, which will be indicated by a mixing of impersonal and personal language about God;
■ language that indicates salvation is based on *one's own effort* to attain *perfection* through a *gradual process*;
■ reasons why he was attracted to the New Age belief system and the needs it is meeting in his life (that is,

meaning in life, ecstatic experience, love, power to change, guidance from beyond, hope of continued existence after death, and so forth).

When appropriate, bring your friend back to the words, phrases, and concepts he has used in his story, then contrast them with biblical concepts: God being a Person, salvation through grace, and the fulfillment that Jesus has given you in your life.

A New Ager is entrenched in a belief system that is opposed to the Christian belief system. The most fundamental difference is in his understanding of God. A New Ager is aware of the reality of the supernatural, but his understanding of God misleads him about the nature of humanity's primary problem (sin) and the solution to that problem. When evangelizing a New Ager, the first aim is to get him to question his present concept of God.

While being careful not to put your New Age friend on the defensive, you do want to provoke his thinking. When it comes to thinking about God, your friend probably believes that his god is a form of universal energy. He will not be concerned about breaking his relationship with such an energy because he believes he is unconditionally extended from it. His concern is to find the best technique for tapping into the power that is contained in that cosmic energy.

You can provoke your friend's thinking by putting the image of God as a Person before him and challenging him to consider its implications. If God is a Person, then—just as in any relationship between two persons—moral issues are involved. Our sin causes a break in our relationship with God, and that break is just as real as a break in a relationship with any person we have wronged. As in any broken relationship, the way to restore our relationship with God is through confessing our guilt and requesting forgiveness. As your New Age friend begins to see the difference between relating to a personal God and to an impersonal oneness, and begins to question his concept of God, the Christian gospel will start to make sense to him.

Tell your New Age friend that if the god is an impersonal force, then that god's laws are like the universal laws of physics or nature, and forgiveness is not possible. The law of karma is precisely that—a law, not a means of receiving grace. If, however, God is a Person, then His law is a moral law. While breaking that law carries severe consequences, forgiveness is possible. Indeed, it is guaranteed through faith in the atoning work of Jesus Christ.

If the god is energy, then that god can be neither concerned about nor aware of our suffering. If God is a Person, though, He can be very much aware of and concerned about our suffering (Exodus 3:7-8). Moreover, through Jesus Christ, God has identified with us in that suffering (Hebrews 4:15), has conquered the source of that suffering (sin and death), and will eventually establish His Kingdom where "He will wipe every tear from their eyes. There will be no more death or mourning or crying or pain" (Revelation 21:4).

If God is a Person, then the love of God has meaning, because love is inherently interpersonal and relational. But if god is an impersonal energy, love loses all meaning, because in the context of such a god, love is only based on the essence of existence. While such a love might be unconditional, it does not affirm our value as persons who believe we are somehow above the oneness of existence. Indeed, such a god would love by absorbing the separateness of the person rather than by affirming it.

Some New Agers might say that they believe their god is personal. What they most likely mean by that, though, is that the impersonal force becomes personal—individualized—in each one of us. We are the impersonal god manifested in a personal form. The question to ask in such a case is: What is God *ultimately*—personal or impersonal?

It is also possible to provoke a New Ager's thinking by pointing out how New Age teaching begins with good news but ends with bad news. If, for example, the god is an impersonal life force from which all existence flows, then the good news is that we are divine, and we cannot be separated from such a god. The bad news is that such an impersonal god is unable to fulfill us as persons. It cannot communicate with us, love us (because love is interpersonal), or empathize with our suffering. Knowing such a god, moreover, becomes a disappearing act for the individual.

The God of Christianity, on the other hand, is supremely Personal. The bad news is that through sin we have alienated ourselves from God and are out of fellowship with Him. The good news is that God as a Person can forgive and love us, which He has done through Jesus Christ. If God is a Person, moreover, then we have value as persons and can look forward to an eternal relationship with Him as we place our faith in the redeeming work of Jesus Christ.

The inclusiveness of the New Age is another form of good news that turns sour. Just as there are many paths to the top of the mountain, New Agers say, so there are many paths to God. The bad news is that salvation becomes a path of striving through innumerable lifetimes to attain some standard of perfection. While the biblical way of salvation begins with the bad news that "all have sinned and fall short of the glory of God," it ends with the good news that we can be "justified freely by his grace through the redemption that came by Christ Jesus" (Romans 3:23-24).

The spiritual technology of the New Age is another example where good news turns to bad news. Spiritual technology is characterized by (1) being based on a force (light, energy, consciousness, and so forth) that we are able to manipulate and (2) guaranteed results if done correctly. The good news is the potential power promised by such a spiritual technology. The bad news is the implications if the results are not produced. Ask your New Age friend if he is realizing all that his spiritual practice promises. If not, what's preventing him from doing so? Wouldn't this reveal a spiritual or attitudinal problem that must be dealt with? Does he know anyone personally who has attained 100 percent mastery over his life or is manifesting 100 percent perfection?

Perhaps the New Ager will blame his suffering on some previous life. In other words, he is paying for his karma. When does he hope to burn off all that karma? Does he know precisely why he is suffering in this lifetime? If not, how can he be assured he won't repeat the same mistake? Has he found grace and forgiveness in karma?

Tim Philibosian, president of Rivendell, a Christian apologetics organization in the Denver area, suggests a good way of provoking doubts in the mind of a New Ager who considers channeled messages to be revelation: "Ask a medium who purportedly is in touch with an ancient Egyptian to identify a simple word, like the Egyptian word for 'air.' And if the entity comes up with a word, check it out."[1]

As your relationship with the New Ager becomes more established, invite him to study the Gospel of John with you. Why a gospel instead of an epistle? Because such a study will help clear up misconceptions your New Age friend might have about Jesus. Also, it's important to get the New Ager thinking about Jesus Christ. The more his thoughts are filled with Jesus, the more likely that he will decide for Him. Pepper your conversations with stories from the gospels about Jesus.

Why study the Gospel of John? First, because John makes it clear in the first chapter that "the Word," which the Greeks understood to be the organizing principle within all things (similar to the New Age god), is actually a Person, not an impersonal force, and that, more specifically, it is Jesus Christ. Second, because John emphasizes the uniqueness of Jesus as the one and only Son of God. Third, because John makes it clear that transformation is the work of God (John 3:3-8) and not of ourselves. Fourth, because John is explicit concerning the fate of the sinner. Fifth, because John articulates the fact that Jesus knew He had come to die and that the purpose of His death was to lay down "his life for the sheep" (John 10:11).

Some final remarks:

■ Don't expect the New Ager to change right away.
■ Pray that the Holy Spirit will work in the heart of your New Age friend to make him receptive to the gospel of Jesus Christ.
■ Keep the idea that God is a Person in the back of your mind at all times. It will serve as a handy guide

for discerning the biblical perspective on most New Age issues.

■ The more your relationship with Jesus is established, the easier it will be to introduce others to Him.

■ Stick to the basic issues of sin and salvation, and avoid becoming defensive or argumentative about side issues.

■ Do not refer to the New Age belief system as satanic. To them, a person making such a remark reveals his own intolerance and ignorance. You may present the biblical evidence, but let them make their own conclusions concerning the source of New Age teaching.

■ Practice evangelizing New Agers.

■ Embody the love of Christ; be a friend.

NOTE

1. Russell Chandler, *Understanding the New Age* (Dallas, TX: Word, Inc., 1988), page 243.

A GLOSSARY
OF NEW AGE TERMS

This glossary can cover only the most essential New Age terms. For a much more complete list, see Bob Larson's *Straight Answers on the New Age.*

CENTERING: A technique that combines YOGA, Zen, body movement, imagery, breathing exercises, relaxation training, and dream work and is intended to "develop a pool of inner stillness."[1] Centering is being practiced in some schools to produce a relaxed mental state in which the person can be more creative and have a better self-image.

CHAKRAS: The seven major energy centers located at various points from the bottom of the spine to the top of the head. Each chakra is formed at the major points where the 72,000 invisible channels (*nadis*) of psychic energy cross with one another. Some associate each chakra with a respective area of the body.

CLAIRVOYANCE: The psychic ability to see something that is not normally visible.

CRYSTALS: New Agers believe that crystals can be programmed with thoughts of health or prosperity and then constantly radiate those messages to effect the desired result.

GAIA HYPOTHESIS: Originally articulated by British scientist James Lovelock and named after the Greek goddess of the earth, the Gaia Hypothesis teaches that the earth acts as a single living organism. While in the scientific community Lovelock's theory represents nothing more than a new way of looking at the earth holistically, New Agers have instilled spiritual significance into the theory. They say the connection between humanity and the earth is on a spiritual level, that the earth is sacred, and that humanity represents Gaia's emergence into consciousness. They also tend to personify the earth by attributing to it personal characteristics.

GLOBALISM: Seeing that many of our planetary problems (acid rain, the greenhouse effect, destruction of the rain forests, the starvation of the poor, and so forth) are caused by separatistic nations looking out for their own interests, New Agers and others say the solution is to be found either in an awareness that is more global in scope or in one-world government. Most New Agers would fall somewhere in between those two extremes, not advocating that nations be abolished but pushing for some kind of world ruling body, such as the United Nations, to be given more authority.

GUIDED IMAGERY: Involves a period of relaxing one's body, quieting one's mind, breathing deeply, and mentally walking through a scene usually supplied by another person. Guided imagery can become a means to get a person in touch with his intuition or introduce him to a spirit-guide.

IRIDOLOGY: Based on the assumption that the iris, the colored part of the eye, is a microcosm of the body and that each part of the iris represents an organ system within the body. By comparing the iris with charts, an iridologist claims to be able to diagnose what's wrong with a patient.[2]

KARMA: The spiritual and moral law of cause and effect. That which you do in either a previous or present lifetime will come back to you in this lifetime or the next. One's karma determines one's destiny in reincarnation.

LOTUS POSITION: This is the standard posture for practicing YOGA. In this posture, the meditator sits on a floor cushion with the right foot over the left thigh and the left foot over the right thigh, the hands extended over the knees with the forefinger and thumb forming a circle on each hand and the eyes either closed or half-closed.

MANTRA: Literally meaning "thought form." It is a thought device on which one concentrates during MEDITATION. Mantras can be either a single syllable or a short phrase and are usually in Sanskrit.

MEDITATION: The process of stilling or quieting the distractions in the mind in order to be attuned to one's *true Self.*

OCCULT: Literally meaning "hidden." Usually refers to hidden or secret powers.

OM: This mantra (see MANTRA) is known as the queen of mantras. It is said to contain all sounds within it and to resonate with the universe as a whole. By sounding OM (sometimes spelled AUM), one becomes attuned to the most fundamental vibration of all things. The goal of meditating on OM is to lose one's individual self in the oneness of the *universal Self.*

REDUCTIONISTIC: A perspective that approaches a problem by fixing an individual part, but disregards the influence that part might have on the whole or the whole might have on that part. The opposite of viewing something holistically.

VALUES CLARIFICATION: A process being used in some public schools to assist students in discovering their values. While on the one hand it encourages people to take a strong stance based on their values, it promotes moral relativity, on the other hand, by saying that moral standards are matters of personal preference and choice.

VISUALIZATION: The meaning of visualization can range from focusing the images of the mind in order to accomplish a goal to the belief that the mind has the power to materialize whatever image it holds.

YOGA: Literally meaning "yoked, union, or to join." The practice of yoga consists of body postures (*asanas*), controlled breathing, and a fixed point for MEDITATION. With some, the goal of yoga is to join one's individual self with the *universal Self* and thereby become liberated from the bondage of this physical world. With others, it is to open the chakras (see CHAKRAS) so the power available through them can be released. Yoga "is best approached as a spiritual discipline rather than a calisthenics."[3]

NOTES
1. Gay Hendricks and Russel Wills, *The Centering Book: Awareness Activities for Children and Adults to Relax the Body and Mind* (New York: Prentice-Hall Press, 1975), pages x and 5.
2. See pages 142-147 in Reisser's *New Age Medicine* for an evaluation of iridology from a medical doctor's perspective.
3. Rick Fields, et al., eds., *Chop Wood, Carry Water* (Los Angeles, CA: J. P. Tarcher, 1984), page 163.

BIBLIOGRAPHY

Christian Resources

Albrecht, Mark. *Reincarnation: A Christian Appraisal.* Downers Grove, IL: InterVarsity Press, 1982.

Ankerberg, John, and John Weldon. *The Facts on Astrology.* Eugene, OR: Harvest House Publishers, 1988.

Chandler, Russell. *Understanding the New Age.* Dallas, TX: Word Publishing, 1988.

Fish, Sharon. "Nursing's New Age." *SCP Newsletter.* Berkeley, CA: Spiritual Counterfeits Project, vol. 14, no. 3, 1989.

Geisler, Norman L., and J. Yutaka Amano. *The Reincarnation Sensation.* Wheaton, IL: Tyndale House Publishers, Inc., 1986.

Groothuis, Douglas R. *Confronting the New Age.* Downers Grove, IL: InterVarsity Press, 1988.

———. *Unmasking the New Age.* Downers Grove, IL: InterVarsity Press, 1986.

Gudel, Joseph P., Robert M. Bowman, and Dan R. Schlesinger. "Reincarnation: Did the Church Suppress It?" *Christian Research Journal* (Summer 1987).

Hexham, Irving, and Karla Poewe. *Understanding Cults and New Religions.* Grand Rapids, MI: Wm. B. Eerdmans Publishing Company, 1986.

Hoyt, Karen, and the Spirital Counterfeits Project. *The New Age Rage.* Old Tappan, NJ: Fleming H. Revell Company, 1987.

Hunt, Dave. *Beyond Seduction.* Eugene, OR: Harvest House Publishers, 1987.

Hunt, Dave, and T. A. McMahon. *The Seduction of Christianity.* Eugene, OR: Harvest House Publishers, 1985.

Korem, Dan. *Powers: Testing the Psychic and Supernatural.* Downers Grove, IL: InterVarsity Press, 1988.

Larson, Bob. *Straight Answers on the New Age.* Nashville, TN: Thomas Nelson Publishers, 1989.

Martin, Walter. *The New Age Cult.* Minneapolis, MN: Bethany House Publishers, 1989.

Miller, Elliot. *A Crash Course on the New Age Movement.* Grand Rapids, MI: Baker Book House, 1989.
Pement, Eric. "The Cry for Crystals." *Cornerstone,* vol. 17, issue 86.
Reisser, Paul C., Teri K. Reisser, and John Weldon. *New Age Medicine: A Christian Perspective on Holistic Health.* Downers Grove, IL: InterVarsity Press, 1987.
Rhodes, Ron. "The Christ of the New Age Movement," part 1, and "The Jesus of the New Age Movement," part 2. *Christian Research Journal* (Summer 1989 and Fall 1989).
Sire, James W. *Shirley MacLaine and the New Age Movement.* Downers Grove, IL: InterVarsity Press, 1988.
Spiritual Counterfeits Project. "Empowering the Self: A Look at the Human Potential Movement." *SCP Journal* (Winter 1981–1982).
———. "Expanding Horizons: Psychical Research and Parapsychology." *SCP Journal* (Winter 1980–1981).
———. "Minding the Store: Influences of the New Age in Business." *SCP Journal,* vol. 9, no. 1, 1989.
———. "Spiritism: The Medium and the Message." *SCP Journal,* vol. 7, no. 1, 1987.
Strohmer, Charles. *What Your Horoscope Doesn't Tell You.* Wheaton, IL: Tyndale House Publishers, Inc., 1988.
Wilson, Clifford, and John Weldon. *Psychic Forces and Occult Shock: A Biblical View.* Chattanooga, TN: Global Publishers, 1987.

Christian Organizations
Christian Research Institute, P. O. Box 500, San Juan Capistrano, CA 92693-0500; (714) 855-9926.
Citizens for Excellence in Education, Box 3200, Costa Mesa, CA 92628; (714) 546-5931.
Spiritual Counterfeits Project, P. O. Box 4308, Berkeley, CA 94704; (415) 540-0300.

General Apologetics Works
Blomberg, Craig. *The Historical Reliability of the Gospels.* Downers Grove, IL: InterVarsity Press, 1987.
Bruce, F. F. *The New Testament Documents: Are They Reliable?* Downers Grove, IL: InterVarsity Press, 1960.
Dyrness, William. *Christian Apologetics in a World Community.* Downers Grove, IL: InterVarsity Press, 1983.
Evans, C. Stephan. *The Quest for Faith: Reason and Mystery as Pointers to God.* Downers Grove, IL: InterVarsity Press, 1986.
France, R. T. *The Evidence for Jesus.* Downers Grove, IL: InterVarsity Press, 1986.
Habermas, Gary. *The Verdict of History: Conclusive Evidence for the Life of Jesus.* Nashville, TN: Thomas Nelson, 1988.
Lewis, C. S. *Mere Christianity.* New York: Macmillan Publishing Co., Inc., 1943.
Lewis, Gordon R. *Testing Christianity's Truth Claims.* Chicago: Moody Press, 1976.
McDowell, Josh. *Evidence That Demands a Verdict.* Arrowhead Springs, CA: Campus Crusade for Christ, 1972.

——. *More Evidence That Demands a Verdict.* Arrowhead Springs, CA: Campus Crusade for Christ, 1975.

Montgomery, John Warwick. *History & Christianity.* Downers Grove, IL: InterVarsity Press, 1964.

Moreland, J. P. *Scaling the Secular City: A Defense of Christianity.* Grand Rapids, MI: Baker Book House, 1987.

Sire, James W. *Scripture Twisting: 20 Ways the Cults Misread the Bible.* Downers Grove, IL: InterVarsity Press, 1980.

——. *The Universe Next Door.* Downers Grove, IL: InterVarsity Press, 1976.

New Age Resources

Body Mind Spirit. Box 701, Providence, RI 02901.

Burns, Litany. *Develop Your Psychic Abilities.* New York: Prentice-Hall Press, 1985.

Campbell, Joseph, with Bill Moyers. *The Power of Myth.* New York: Doubleday, 1988.

Capra, Fritjof. *The Tao of Physics.* Berkeley, CA: Shambhala, 1975.

——. *The Turning Point.* New York: Simon and Schuster, 1982.

Ferguson, Marilyn. *The Aquarian Conspiracy: Personal and Social Transformation in the 1980s.* Los Angeles, CA: J. P. Tarcher, Inc., 1980.

Fields, Rick, Peggy Taylor, Rex Weyler, and Rick Ingrasci. *Chop Wood, Carry Water: A Guide to Finding Spiritual Fulfillment in Everyday Life.* Los Angeles, CA: J. P. Tarcher, Inc., 1984.

Fox, Matthew. *The Coming of the Cosmic Christ.* San Francisco, CA: Harper & Row, Publishers, 1988.

Gawain, Shakti. *Creative Visualization.* New York: Bantam Books, 1982.

Hendricks, Gay, and Russel Wills. *The Centering Book: Awareness Activities for Children and Adults to Relax the Body and Mind.* New York: Prentice-Hall Press, 1975.

Hubbard, Barbara Marx. *The Evolutionary Journal: A Personal Guide to a Positive Future.* San Francisco, CA: Evolutionary Press, 1982.

Kautz, William H., and Melanie Branon. *Channeling: The Intuitive Connection.* San Francisco, CA: Harper & Row, Publishers, 1987.

Klimo, Jon. *Channeling: Investigations on Receiving Information from Paranormal Sources.* Los Angeles, CA: J. P. Tarcher, Inc., 1987.

Krieger, Dolores. *The Therapeutic Touch: How to Use Your Hands to Help or to Heal.* New York: Prentice-Hall, 1979.

MacLaine, Shirley. *Dancing in the Light.* New York: Bantam Books, 1985.

——. *Going Within: A Guide for Inner Transformation.* New York: Bantam Books, 1989.

——. *Out on a Limb.* New York: Bantam Books, 1983.

Muller, Robert. *New Genesis: Shaping a Global Spirituality.* Garden City, NY: Doubleday & Company, Inc., 1982.

New Age Journal. 342 Western Ave., Brighton, MA 02135.

Russell, Peter. *The Global Brain: Speculations on the Evolutionary Leap to Planetary Consciousness.* Los Angeles, CA: J. P. Tarcher, Inc., 1983.

Satin, Mark. *New Age Politics: Healing Self and Society.* New York: Dell, 1978.

Siegel, Bernie S. *Love, Medicine, and Miracles.* New York: Harper & Row, Publishers, 1986.

Spangler, David. *Revelation: The Birth of a New Age*. Elgin, IL: Lorian
Press, 1976.

Wilde, Stuart. *The Force*. Taos, NM: White Dove International, Inc.,
1984.

Zukav, Gary. *The Dancing Wu Li Masters*. New York: William Morrow
and Company, Inc., 1979.

——. *The Seat of the Soul*. New York: Simon and Schuster, 1989.

Secular Resources

Gardner, Martin. *The New Age: Notes of a Fringe Watcher*. Buffalo, NY:
Prometheus Books, 1988.

Hines, Terence. *Pseudoscience and the Paranormal*. Buffalo, NY:
Prometheus Books, 1988.

National Research Council. Daniel Druckman and John A. Swets, eds.
Enhancing Human Performance: Issues, Theories, and Techniques.
Washington, DC: National Academy Press, 1988.

**FOR A FREE CATALOG OF
NAVPRESS BOOKS & BIBLE STUDIES,
CALL TOLL FREE 800-366-7788 (USA)
or 1-416-499-4615 (CANADA)**